A Treasury of Flannelboard Stories

By Jeanette Graham Bay

Alleyside Press

Fort Atkinson, Wisconsin

Published by Alleyside Press, an imprint of Highsmith Press
Highsmith Press
W5527 Highway 106
P.O. Box 800
Fort Atkinson, Wisconsin 53538-0800
1-800-558-2110

The paper used in this publication meets the minimum requirements of
American National Standard for Information Science — Permanence of Paper
for Printed Library Material. ANSI/NISO Z39.48-1992.

Library of Congress Cataloging in Publication
    Bay, Jeanette Graham
        A treasury of flannelboard stories / Jeanette Graham Bay.
            p.   cm.
        Includes bibliographical references.
        ISBN 0-917846-51-6 (alk. paper)
            1. Flannelgraphs. 2. Children's stories. 3. Storytelling.
        I. Title.
    LB1043.62.B39 1995
    371.3'35--dc20   94-43639
                                                                CIP

Contents

Introduction

There is an old Chinese Proverb,

When I hear, I forget
When I see, I remember
When I do, I learn.

I feel the flannelboard is a great teaching tool. It can be used in the classroom, and parents and grandparents can use it in the home. Children themselves love to color the reproduced patterns, cut them out, put flannel or velcro on the back and tell the story as it is written in the book, or make up their own story. This helps to bring out a child's creativity and imagination.

Most of the knowledge children absorb is best acquired through exploration and through experimentation. Learning comes from seeing and asking questions. Learning occurs through use of the senses—seeing, hearing, touching, smelling and tasting. These all give us a clue to the nature of the world we live in. Children need to experience these senses. The flannelboard uses three of these senses—seeing, hearing and touching.

Children learn by doing. They can act out frustrations, and use flannelboard patterns to tell their stories. A shy child will open up when playing a part in a game or story. They will take an active part in placing pictures on the flannelboard and expressing themselves verbally.

When a child is listening and seeing a flannelboard story being told, he or she has a chance to show and tell and do some problem solving. A teacher can start a story and have the child finish it in his or her own way. A child may tell the same story over and over again. Repetition is stimulating for a young child.

A teacher or parent wants to build curiosity, independence, creativity and kindness in a child. Positive feelings accompany successful communication. Learning should be fun. Children at an early age learn through play. Many different topics can be introduced through the use of the flannelboard. The flannelboard story can be playtime activity. Songs and accompanying pictures can be fun. Guessing missing objects from a group of pictures, dance movements, rhythm instruments can all be introduced through flannelboard pictures. Counting and classification skills are easily learned with pictures. Even science experiments can be shown through pictures on the flannelboard. Charades and play-acting activities can be used with the flannelboard, and they are a great way to facilitate action and participation games.

Children grow and develop at different speeds. Four developmental areas are: *physical*—motor growth, *emotional*—feelings, *intellectual*—thinking and reasoning, and *social*—getting along with others and interacting. Each of these child development goals can be introduced with the flannelboard story.

1. Physical—acting out a story, using small motor skills in manipulating the pictures on the flannelboard.
2. Emotional—a child will use self expression when telling a story. Feelings and personality can be expressed.
3. Intellectual—a child can memorize a story and tell it, or make up a new story. Thinking and problem solving are involved.
4. Social growth—a child is building confidence to stand in front of class and tell a story. A child will interact with others.

To use a flannelboard story book, I first reproduce the pictures, color them with markers or crayons, cut them out, and either laminate or cover them with clear contact sheets (to protect the picture). I'll then add velcro or felt on the back of each picture. There is a great item called Quick Stick Felt that works well. This product is manufactured by the Felters Company, and sold in many craft stores.

When copying patterns to use with the flannelboard, check to see if a picture would work better if it was made completely out of felt instead of paper with a felt backing. Use the paper picture as the pattern for the felt picture. I use different colored felt squares and paste the picture together, such as a person—flesh-colored body, blond hair, blue eyes, red dress, etc. Some stories just work better when felt pieces are used. Felt sticks to felt, therefore, in stories when clothing is changed or objects need to be placed on top of objects, felt is ideal.

If you don't have a flannelboard, make one. They can be easily made with a wood frame or use a piece of heavy cardboard and cover with felt or flannel. Just tack or staple it on. Most items needed for the flannelboard can be found in any craft store. Many library suppliers also offer flannelboard equipment and resources such as boards and easels. Highsmith lists a variety of materials in their School & Classroom Catalog. (Call 1-800-558-2110 for a free catalog.)

I find it's convenient to always put the picture patterns for each story in an individual manila envelope and label it.

When telling a flannelboard story or any story, try to memorize it or really know it so well that you can tell it smoothly and without hesitation. Have the pictures in the right order to easily place them on the flannelboard. Keep the children's attention and at times have them add or remove a picture. I prefer to sit in a chair to the left or right of the flannelboard, which is placed on an easel stand. This way I am slightly higher than the children, who are sitting on the floor in front of me.

I try to keep the flannelboard story short and simple to make it easy to tell. Each story is a special learning and fun experience for the child. Your local library carries many story books for the young child. Many of them may be used with the flannelboard.

Please enjoy using my book. I certainly enjoyed writing it.

Recommended further reading

Some additional educational/instructional books I would like to mention are:

Pre-Kindergarten Discoveries by James Hoffman and Joan Hoffman (Minneapolis: T.S. Denison, 1966. 104 pp.).

Children discover and thrive in a flexible, creative, pleasant, relaxing and busy atmosphere where there is a minimal of don'ts and much to do. Children discover in an atmosphere that promotes self understanding. The school has a balanced program of quiet and active work and play throughout the day. Positive curriculum must be maintained. A child's curiosity should be satisfied by the process of discovery. This book is rich in discovery activities from cooking, block building, science experiments to art and fingerplays.

Games for Learning by Peggy Kaye (New York: Farrar, Straus & Giroux, 1991. 256 pp.).

Has many ideas that can be adapted in a flannelboard story or used with the flannelboard.

Kids Are Worth It by Barbara Coloroso (New York: Morrow, 1994. 253 pp.) and *You and Your Child's Self-Esteem* by James M. Harris (New York: Warner, 1990. 224 pp.).

These are books that give many insights into how and why young children learn and ways we as parents and teachers can instill the love of learning into a child.

The New Read Aloud Handbook (New York: Viking, 1989. 352 pp.) and *Hey! Listen to This:Stories to Read Aloud* (New York: Viking Children's Books, 1992. 240 pp.) by Jim Trelease.

This book has many stories for the young child that could be used with the flannelboard. The story for the young child can be short but still full of information and adventure.

The New Handbook for Storytellers by Caroline F. Bauer (Chicago: American Library Association, 1993. 650 pp.).

Bauer shows parents, teachers, librarians, and volunteers how to use a variety of media, including film, music, crafts, puppetry, and even magic. It is a complete guide to successful storytelling. The author writes there have been so many wonderful books published for children that everyone needs to know about them. There is a section on family storytelling and many, many stories, poems, songs, riddles, jokes and patterns. Therefore it will be many years before anyone becomes bored with this resource.

The Flannel Board Storytelling Book by Judy Sierra (New York: Wilson, 1987. 216 pp.).

Flannelboard storytelling is an art widely practiced by teachers and librarians. Countless generations of storytellers have used figures and drawings both to entertain their listeners and to help themselves remember their tales. One may make more direct contact to listeners when using the flannelboard. This book contains 36 stories, songs and poems from many countries with diverse cultures.

Multicultural Folktales: Stories to Tell Young Children by Judy Sierra and Robert Kaminiski (Phoenix: Oryx Press 1991. 136 pp.).

Folktales come to us through the oral tradition so it is natural that we look to this source for stories to tell aloud to children. A country or area of origin is given for each folktale in this book, though this merely indicates the place in which one particular version of the story was collected. There are 25 stories and rhymes in this book arranged in order from those suitable for the youngest to the oldest. It is easier to tell stories to young children if they can participate verbally and physically in the storytelling.

Teeny-Tiny Folktales by Jean Warren (Everett, WA: Warren Publishing House, 1987. 80 pp.).

This book has endeavored to modernize the folktales to please young children. That is, to shorten and adapt them. Folktales are found in all cultures around the world.

The Story-Tellers Start-Up Book by Margaret Read MacDonald (Little Rock, AR: August House, 1993.).

This book intends to convince you that preparing stories is easy and that telling them is such fun you will never want to stop once you have started. Everyone has a story to tell. Storytelling comes from the heart, not the head, and nothing should keep us from the exhilaration and sheer pleasure of telling a story.

Felt Board Fun for Everyday and Holidays by Liz and Dick Wilmes (Elgin, IL: Building Blocks, 1984. 244 pp.).

This book has been written and illustrated to help you make your feltboard an indispensable part of your classroom. The book contains units on the holidays and seasons, the body, senses, animals, food, colors, shapes, letters, numbers and others.

Filled with many ideas and activities that let the children become involved and helps them learn basic concepts, think creatively and enjoy holidays.

Stories that Stick on the Flannelboard by Louise Binder Scott (Minneapolis: T.S. Denison, 1984.).

This book has seasonal stories that are easily told, with patterns, that are full of fun.

For Reading Out Loud by Margaret Mary Kimmel and Elizabeth Segel (New York: Dell, 1991. 356 pp.).

This book is a guide to sharing books with children. Who curled up with you and read to you as a child? Who helped you feel good about yourself? Who gave you the feeling that books are good and reading is good and can be a favorite thing to do? Reading aloud to children from literature is widely acknowledged among experts to be the most effective, as well as the simplest and least expensive, way to foster in children a lifelong love of books and reading. This book is full of short read-aloud stories and suggested listening age levels for each story.

Story Programs: A Source Book of Materials by Carolyn Sue Peterson and Brenny Hall (Metuchen, NJ: Scarecrow Press, 1980. 300 pp.).

This book is designed to aid in conducting story programs for young children. This book contains finger plays and action stories; verses, songs, and stories for the flannelboard with patterns. A story program can take place anywhere, in a library, school room, playground, Sunday school, child care center, or in a home.

Pre-school Story Hour by Vardine Moore (Metuchen, NJ: Scarecrow Press, 1972.).

Young children need to feel at home in their ever widening world. This can be achieved happily and effectively in a well organized and thoughtfully planned story hour for preschoolers. Vocabularies and communication skills develop readily.

Kids Stuff: Book of Reading & Language Arts for the Primary Grades by Imogene Forte and Joy MacKenzie (Nashville, TN: Incentive Publications, 1989. 240 pp.).

Kindergarten and nursery school language arts, science, social studies, math, art, music are included in this book. The book provides teachers with creative activities for use with pupils. Some ideas will be appropriate for capturing the interest of the immature child while others will provide incentive and challenge the more advanced and gifted youngsters. A part of the book provides hints and aids to the teacher so that she can make more effective use of her time and enjoy a more creative and worthwhile learning experience with her pupils.

The Family Storytelling Handbook by Anne Pellowski (New York: Macmillan, 1987. 160 pp.).

Anecdotes, rhymes, handkerchiefs, paper, and other objects to enrich your family traditions. This book shows how you can use a multitude of materials around the home to make storytelling and play fun, even flannelboard story fun.

Action Verse for Early Childhood by Margaret Hillert (Cleveland: Modern Curriculum Press, 1984.).

This book has a treasure of poems and action games. Many of which can be adapted for use with the flannelboard. Many are seasonal oriented.

Creative Encounters: Activities to Expand Children's Responses to Literature by Anne T. Polkingharn and Catherine Toohey (Englewood, CO: Libraries Unlimited, 1983. 138 pp.).

The activities and exercises in this book are designed to allow children to express their creativity. The child's imagination is guided by responses to the author's ideas. We encourage children to develop personal literary tastes, to read books they enjoy and to discover new titles and authors.

Children Tell Stories: A Teaching Guide by Martha Hamilton and Mitch Weiss (Katonah, NY: Richard C. Owen Publications, 1990. 225 pp.).

One doesn't need props or costumes to keep a large group of kids quiet and entertained. With only slight encouragement, they can find enjoyment in a participatory story that would involve them. A humorous tale found the listeners beside themselves with laughter, a quieter, more poignant tale was told and a hush would descend over the group. As storytellers, we have the ability to make the here and now disappear for our listeners, and take them on journeys full of wonder and enchantment. This book is about how to teach children to tell stories.

Eye Winker- Tom Tinker- Chin Chopper by Tom Glazer (New York: Doubleday, 1973.).

This book features 50 musical fingerplays with piano arrangements and guitar chords. It has become quite clear that almost all healthy children have a deep need for dramatic expression. Through the fun of acting out these songs, children are learning and growing.

1 The Travels of Ladybug

This story teaches about different types of transportation.

Pictures needed for this story:

Ladybug	Billy
Timmy with sweater	hat
school bus	motorcycle
Sarah	wind
car	Mary
train	purse
Hannah (pocket)	airplane
Andrew (collar)	boat
big fish	

Ladybug snuggled up in the sleeve of **Timmy's** sweater as Timmy rode the **bus** to school.

At school **Ladybug** flew out the window and landed in Sarah's hair. **Sarah** was just getting in her **car** to go to the train station. So **Ladybug** went along for a ride in the car.

At the train station **Ladybug** flew out the car window and landed right in **Hannah's pocket.** Hannah was just getting on the **train.**

The train started to chug, chug along. It was a long ride and **Ladybug** was tired. She went to sleep in Hannah's pocket.

When **Hannah** was getting off the **train,** **Ladybug** flew out of her pocket and landed on **Billy's hat.** Billy was getting on his **motorcycle** to drive to the airport.

Ladybug had to hang on for dear life because **Billy** was driving fast, and the **wind** was blowing hard against his **hat.**

Ladybug breathed a sigh of relief when **Billy** parked his **motorcycle** at the airport. She quickly flew away and landed in **Mary's purse.**

Mary was getting on the **airplane. Ladybug** took a nap in **Mary's purse** on the **airplane.**

When **Ladybug** woke up they were back on the ground. She flew out of **Mary's purse** and landed on **Andrew's collar.**

Andrew was getting on a big **boat. Ladybug** liked the boat ride but after a while decided to fly off **Andrew's collar** and explore.

Ladybug landed in the water. A **big fish** opened its mouth and swallowed **Ladybug.**

Ladybugs

Mary

Hannah

Purse

11

Billy

Andrew

Hat

Sarah

Tim

Car

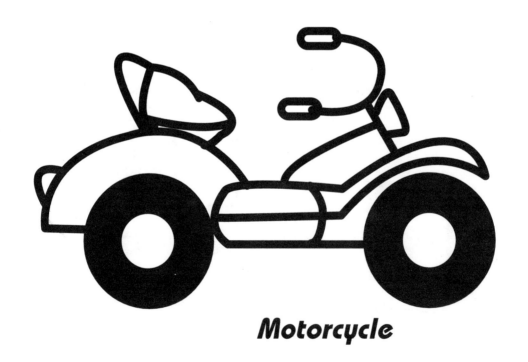

Motorcycle

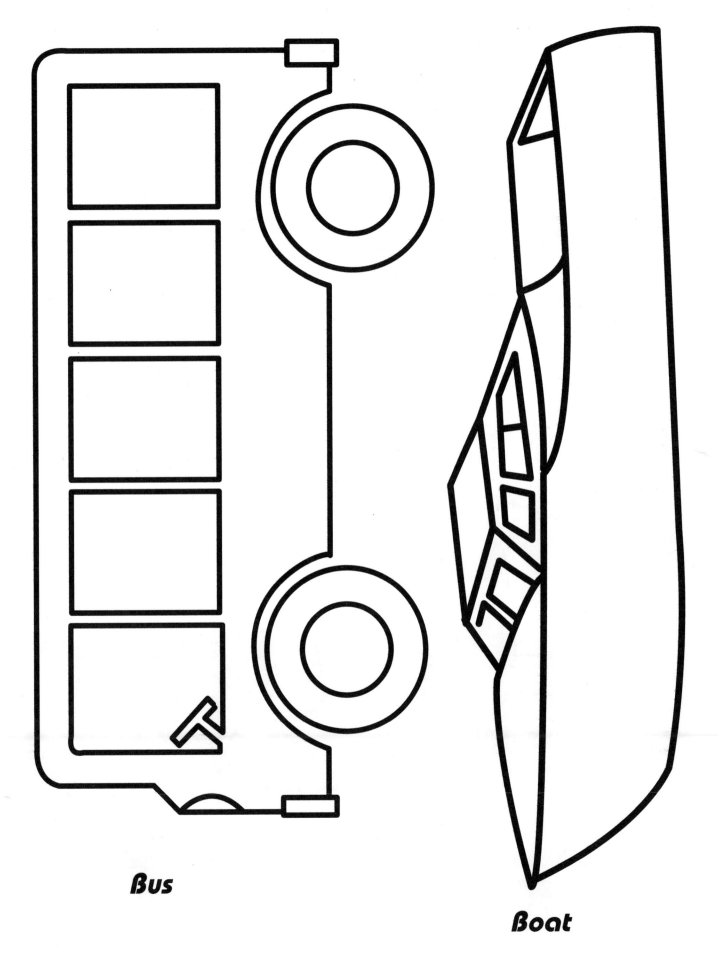

Bus

Boat

15

Airplane

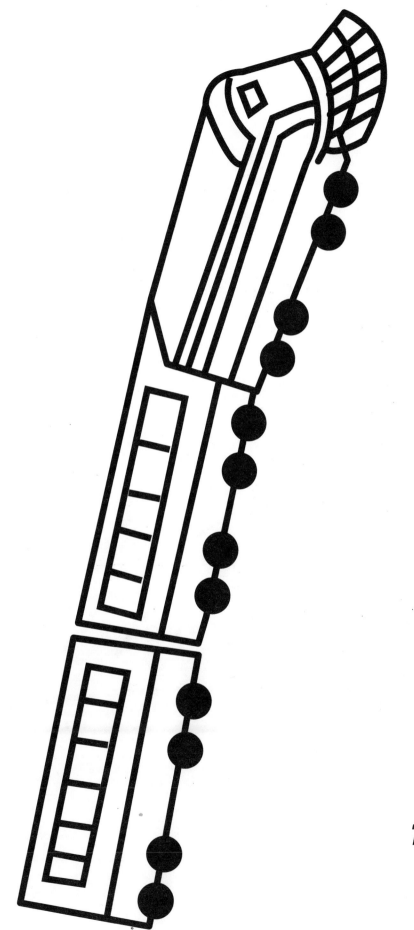

Train

Fish

Wind

2 Shapes and More Shapes

This story teaches about shapes and spatial concepts. Ready-made shapes can be used, but I prefer to make the shapes out of felt because it sticks together better. Furniture and people shapes may also be added as well as other shapes and other buildings.

Pictures needed for this story:

Shawn	toy car
Olivia	middle size square
hammer and nails	large triangle
large square	middle size triangle
4 small squares	large circle
long rectangle	small rectangle

Olivia wanted a playhouse. One day she asked her brother, **Shawn,** to help her build one.

"What will we build it with?" she asked Shawn.

"Let's ask Dad for some wood and a **hammer and nails**," said Shawn.

Dad gave **Shawn** and **Olivia** several pieces of wood in different sizes, some nails and a hammer. Shawn started to build the playhouse. First he made a **large square** frame. He divided this into **four small square rooms**.

"I want a kitchen and a living room downstairs and two bedrooms upstairs," said Olivia.

Shawn used the **large triangle** on top of the **large square** for the roof. He then put a **long rectangle** beside the large square for the chimney. Olivia put a **small rectangle** in the middle of the large square for the door. She put a **small square** in each room for a window. Shawn added a **large circle** in the middle of the large triangle on the roof for a window.

"I like this playhouse, **Shawn**," said **Olivia**.

"Let's make a garage beside the house," suggested Shawn. "I can put my play **car** in it."

Shawn used a **middle-size square** for the garage and put a **triangle** on top for the roof. Olivia added a **square** door.

"Thanks," said **Shawn**.

"I like my playhouse. Let's play in it now," replied Olivia.

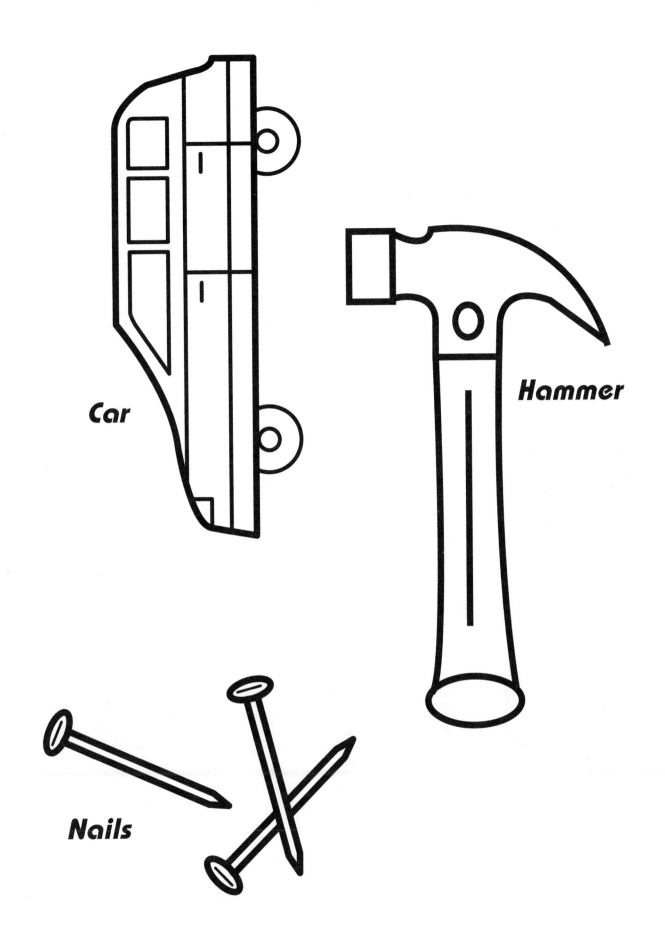

Car

Hammer

Nails

Shawn   **Olivia**

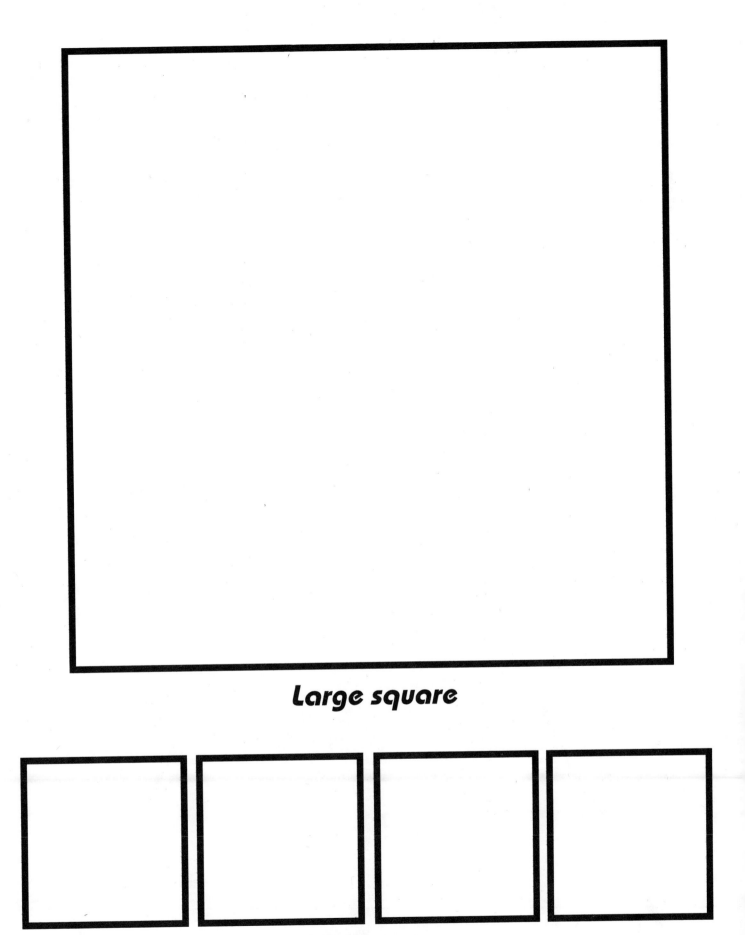

Large square

Small square

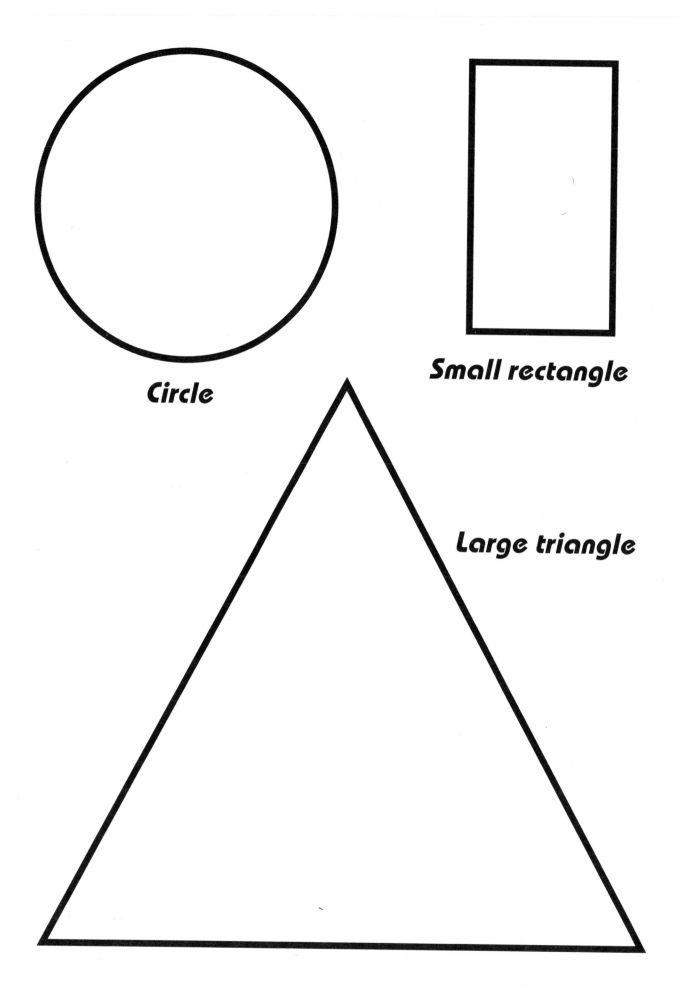

Circle

Small rectangle

Large triangle

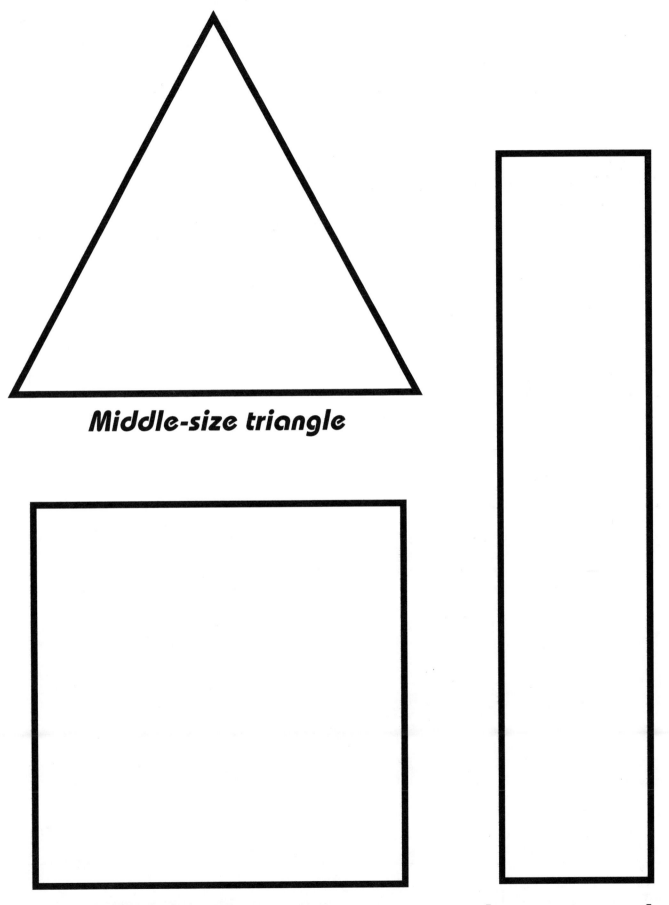

Middle-size triangle

Middle-size square

Long rectangle

3 Worm Wilma's Tail

This story teaches about worms and some animals.

Pictures needed for this story:

worm	deer
tail pieces	raccoon
apple trees	Timmy
whole apple &	
apples with pieces	
missing	

Worm Wilma lived all her life in an apple **orchard**. She was a beautiful **worm,** as worms go. Worm Wilma had an extra long slimy **tail.** She was very proud of that long **tail.**

One day **Worm Wilma** crawled and slithered along until she found the biggest, juiciest red **apple** in the **orchard.** She was hungry so she went chomp, chomp and ate a big hole in the apple.

"I might as well eat slowly since it's going to take a long time to get through to the other side of this apple," thought Worm Wilma.

While **Worm Wilma** was eating her way through the **apple, Deer Daisy** wandered out of the nearby woods and found that big red juicy apple. She took a bite out of it and bit off a tiny piece of **Worm Wilma's tail**.

"Ouch," yelled **Worm Wilma.** "That's my **tail**."

Deer Daisy walked away munching on the piece the **apple**.

As **Worm Wilma** chomped and chomped on that big red juicy **apple**, it started to grow dark. She fell asleep in the apple.

It so happened that **Raccoon Roger** was wandering around that same night looking for food. He saw that big red juicy apple, and he took a bite out of it. He also bit off a piece of **Worm Wilma's tail**.

"Ouch," cried **Worm Wilma** waking up, "That's my **tail**." **Raccoon Roger** walked away munching on his piece of the apple.

"I'd better get out of this apple fast or my **tail** will be all gone," exclaimed **Worm Wilma**.

The next day, as **Worm Wilma** was crawling out of the **apple, Timmy** came looking for a big red juicy apple to eat. He picked up that same apple that **Worm Wilma**, **Deer Daisy**, and **Raccoon Roger** had eaten and said, "This is a nice big red juicy apple, but it has a worm in it." He threw the apple back on the ground and found another one.

Worm Wilma breathed a sigh of relief, "I don't want to lose any more of my **tail**." And she crawled away from that nice big red juicy **apple** glad to be safe at last.

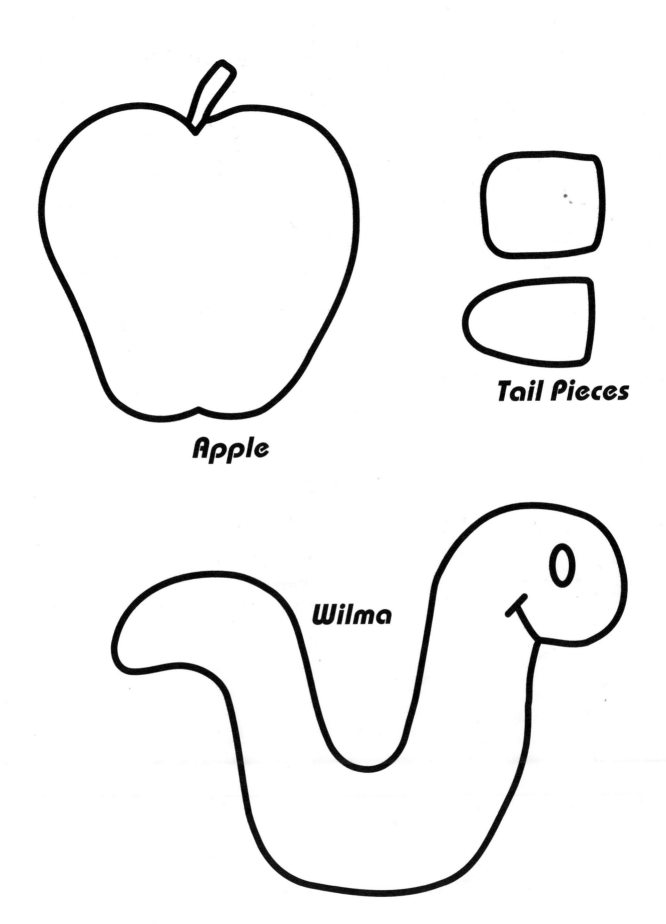

Apple

Tail Pieces

Wilma

Apple Tree

Timmy

Apples with pieces missing

Deer Daisy

Racoon Roger

30

4 Farmer Tom

This story teaches about big and little farm animals, and about some animal products. This is a story the children will want to tell themselves. Other animals may be used.

Pictures needed for this story:

Farmer Tom	dog & puppies
Wife Betty	cat & kittens
Dad	sleigh
Teddy	cookies & milk
Matthew	milk carton
cow & calf	egg carton
hens & chicks	bacon
horse & colt	tractor & wagon
turkey	barn & silo
pig & piglet	milk truck
sheep & lambs	sweater & hat

Teddy and **Matthew** were cousins. They often played together. One day Teddy asked his **father** to take them to visit the farm.

When they arrived at the farm, they saw a big **barn** and a **silo** (a place where grain is stored). In front of the barn was a big green **tractor** with a **wagon** full of hay behind it.

Farmer Tom and his wife, **Betty**, saw them arrive and walked over to welcome them.

"Hello," said Teddy and Matthew together. "Can we visit your farm?"

"I'd be happy to show you around," said Farmer Tom.

"When your tour is finished come into the house. We can have some milk and cookies," said the farmer's wife, Betty.

That was the beginning of their day at the farm. Teddy and Matthew saw **cows** and **calves**.

"We have machines that milk the cows twice a day. The **milk** truck picks up the **milk** and takes it to the milk plant where it is pasteurized and put into cartons or bottles. When you buy milk in the store, you'll know where it comes from," said Farmer Tom.

"Moo, moo," said the cows.

They saw **hens** and **chicks**.

"Chickens give us **eggs**," said Farmer Tom. "We collect eggs everyday, sort them and take them to the store to sell."

"Cluck, cluck," said the chickens.

Teddy and Matthew saw **horses** and **colts**.

"Horses sometimes help on the farm by pulling wagons. Horses are also fun to ride," said Farmer Tom. "In the winter we have **sleigh** rides for children with the horses pulling the sleigh."

"Neigh, neigh," said the horses.

They saw **sheep** and **lambs**.

"We get **wool** for **clothes** from the sheep," said Farmer Tom. He showed some wool that had been sheared from the sheep.

"Baa, baa," said the sheep.

Teddy and Matthew saw **pigs** and **piglets**.

"We get our good hams and **bacon** from the pigs," said Farmer Tom. "Do you have bacon for breakfast?" he asked.

"Squeal, squeal" said the pigs.

All of a sudden two **turkeys** ran around the barn chasing each other, making a loud "gobble, gobble."

"They better watch out, Thanksgiving is coming," Farmer Tom said.

They saw **cats** and **kittens**.

"The cats help us keep the mouse population down and they drink the cows' milk," said Farmer Tom. "They make nice pets, too."

"Meow, meow," said the cats.

When Teddy, Matthew, Dad and Farmer Tom were on their way into the house, they saw two **dogs** and some **puppies**.

"The dogs are good pets and sometimes help us round up the sheep," said Farmer Tom. "They are good watch dogs."

"Bow wow," said the dogs.

In the kitchen Farmer Tom's wife, **Betty**, gave them some **milk and cookies**.

When it was time to go home **Teddy** and **Matthew** and **Dad** said good-bye and thanked **Farmer Tom** and **Betty** for a nice visit and tour of their farm.

How many different animals did you see on the farm?

Betty

Farmer Tom

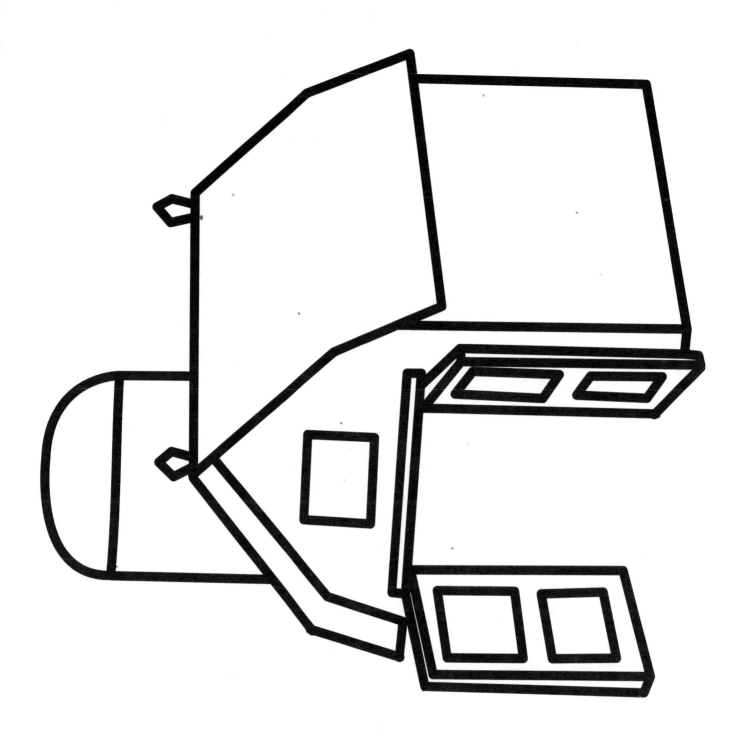

Barn & silo

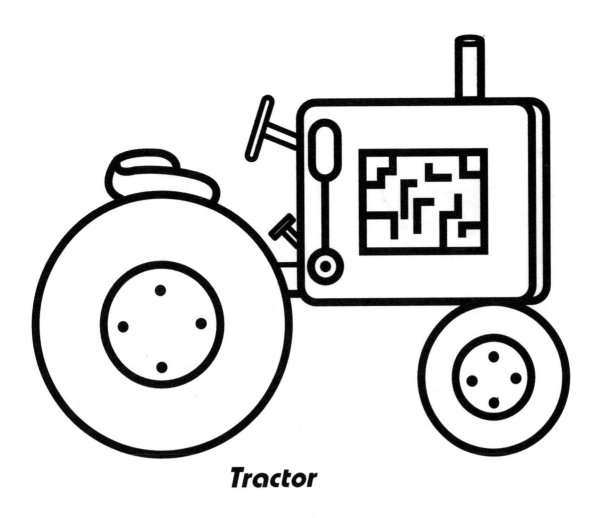

Tractor

Wagon

Teddy

Matthew

Dad

Cat & kitten

Dog & puppy

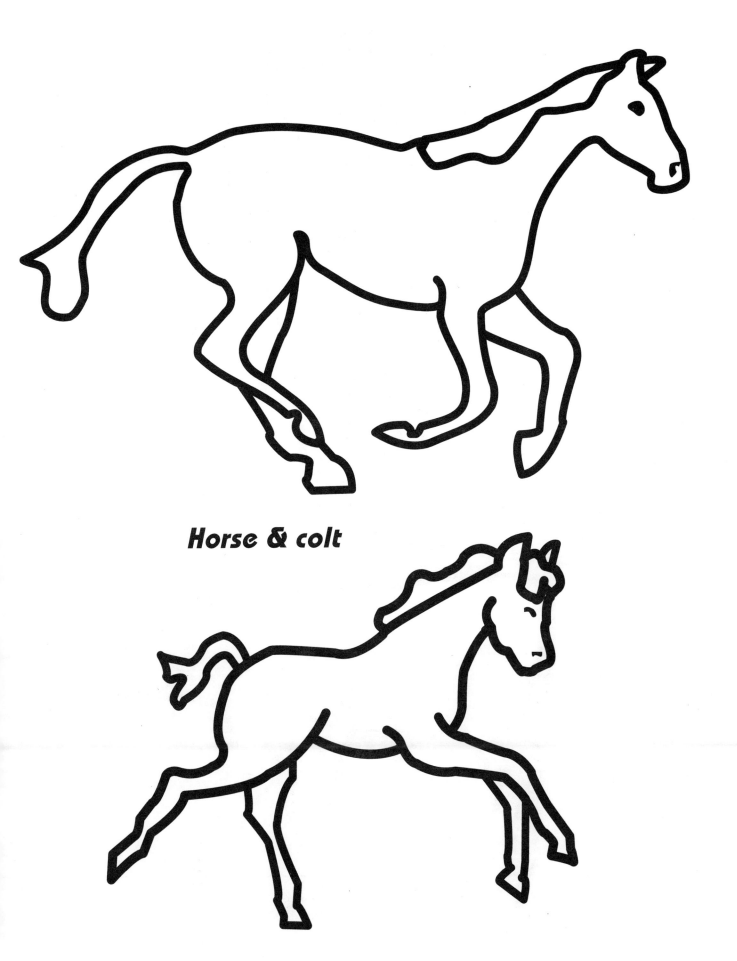

Horse & colt

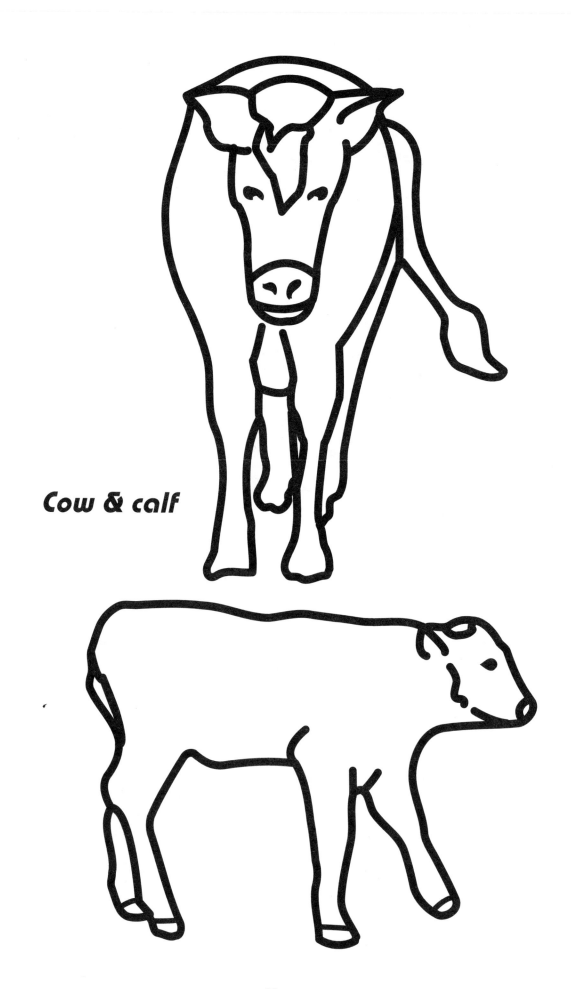

Cow & calf

Pig & piglet

Sheep & lamb

Turkey

Hen & chicks

Milk & cookies

Eggs

Milk

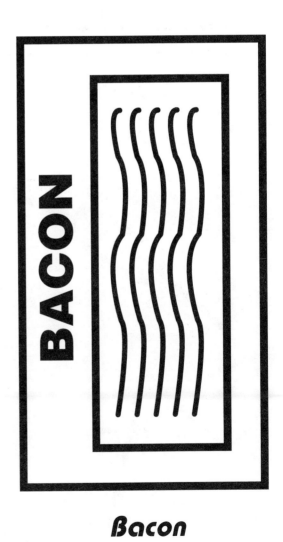

Bacon

Sleigh

**Wool hat
& sweater**

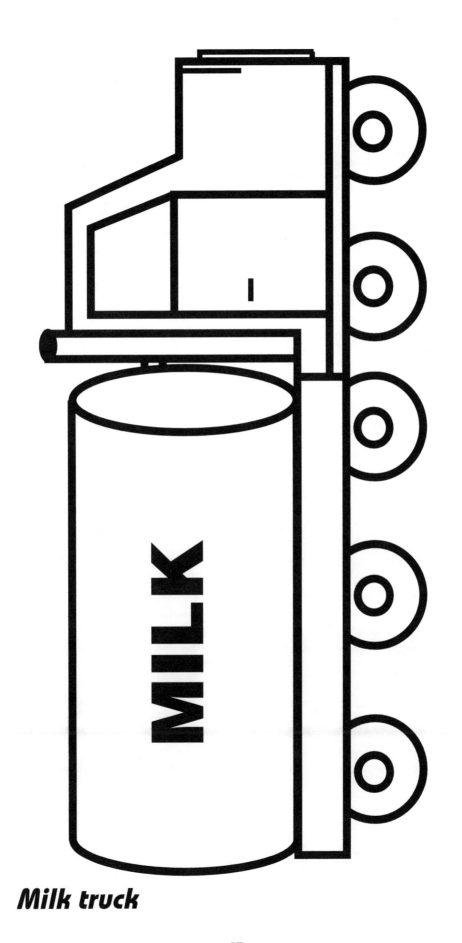

Milk truck

5 Grandma's Secret

This story teaches problem solving.

Pictures needed:

Grandma	closet
Mother	blanket chest
Emily	store counters
Tim	store front
bag	tie
dinosaur	flashlight
doll house	telephone
bed	Asher
Christmas tree	bush

Grandma had a secret. **Christmas** was coming and there was an air of excitement around the house. Maybe Grandma's secret had something to do with Christmas.

Grandma left the house everyday at noon and didn't come home until 5 o'clock. And she was always carrying a **big bag** in her arms when she came home. She took the big bag to her room and hid it. Where? I don't know, but **I** sneaked in her room once and looked. I looked under her **bed**. It wasn't there.

"Maybe it's a dinosaur," **I** said to **Asher**, my friend at school.

"A dinosaur wouldn't fit in a bag, **Emily**," he said.

"Maybe it is a baby dinosaur," I said.

The next day when my **grandmother** left the house at noon, **I** followed her. She walked along the sidewalk, rather fast, and I had to skip to keep up. Once she started to turn around, but I jumped behind a **bush** so she didn't see me.

Grandma went into a **department store** and I followed her.

We walked past the **shoe section**, and past the **jewelry section**. Every once in a while Grandma would look back, but I would hide behind a **counter** so she didn't see me. Then, all of a sudden, I looked

around and couldn't see her. Where did she go? I ran up and down the aisles, but she had disappeared. I walked back home very disappointed.

At 5 o'clock, sure enough, **Grandma** came home carrying a **big bag**. She took it to her room and hid it. Where? I don't know, but **I** sneaked into her room to look. I looked in her **closet**. It wasn't there.

"Maybe it's a doll house," **I** told **Asher** the next day at school.

"A doll house wouldn't fit in the bag," he said.

"It could be a tiny doll house," I said.

One day, my **mother** and **I** went to the same department store I'd seen my grandother visit. We were shopping for Christmas gifts. We bought a **flowered tie** for Grandpa. We bought a **flashlight** for Dad. Then, we went to the toy department to buy a gift for my brother, Tim. Who do you think we saw behind the **counter** selling toys? It was my **Grandma**.

"Hi, Grandma," I called. "Do you work here?"

"I'm just helping out at Christmas time," Grandma said.

As soon as Mother and I arrived home, **I** went and called my friend, **Asher**, and told him about my grandmother.

"She works in the toy department and I just know she has toys in the big bags when she comes home," I explained.

On Christmas morning, sure enough, there were the toys Grandma had carried home in her big bag. There really was a **baby dinosaur** for my **brother, Tim**, and a small **doll house** for **me**.

Do you know where Grandma hid the big bags of toys so I wouldn't find them? She hid them in her **blanket chest** by her bed. That's where I was going to look next.

Grandma

Emily

Mother

Tim

Asher

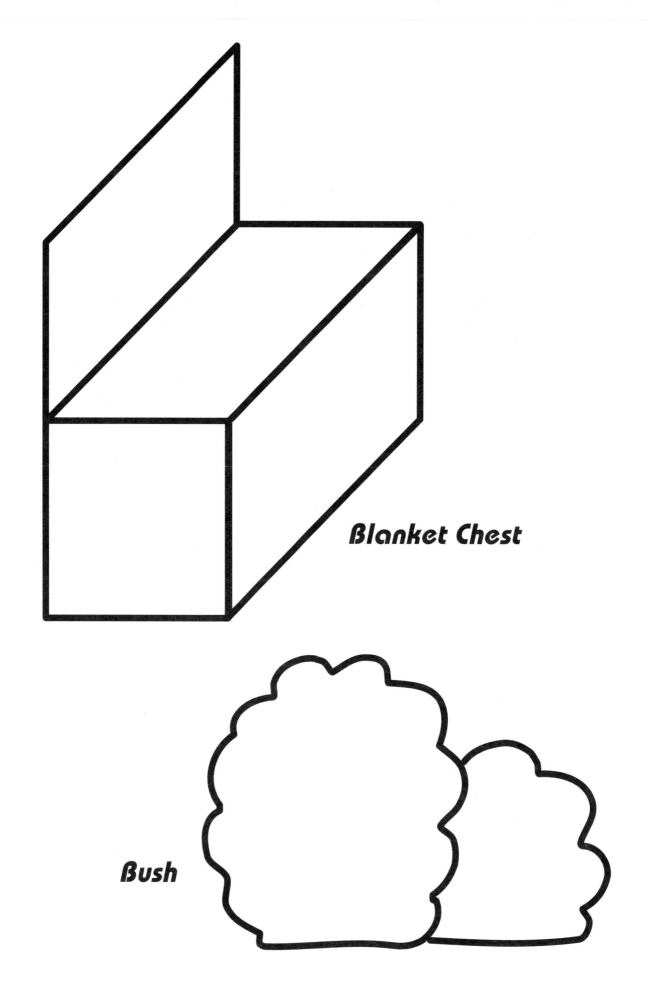

Blanket Chest

Bush

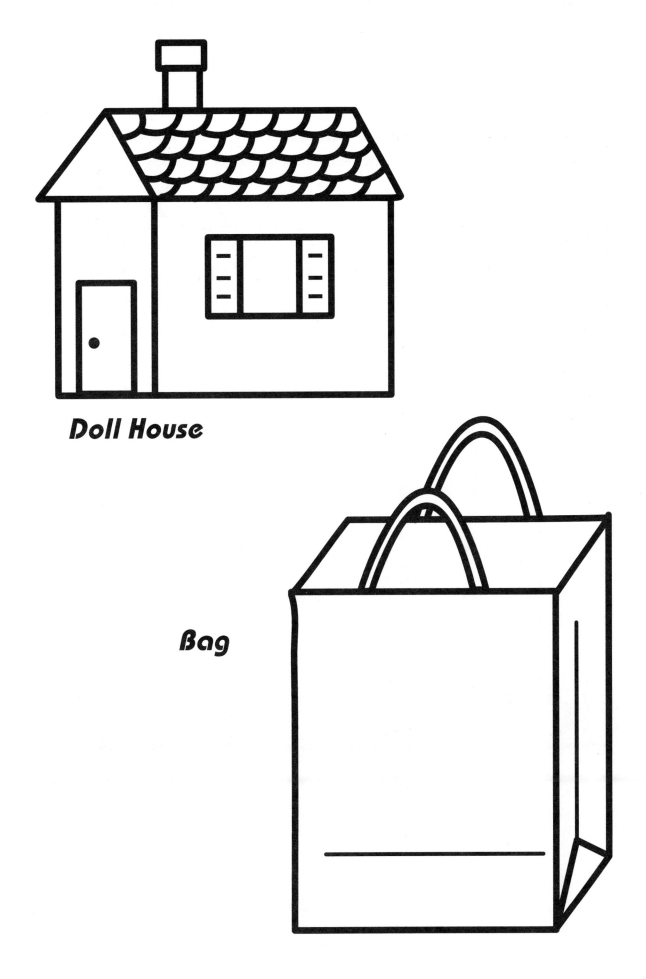

Doll House

Bag

Closet

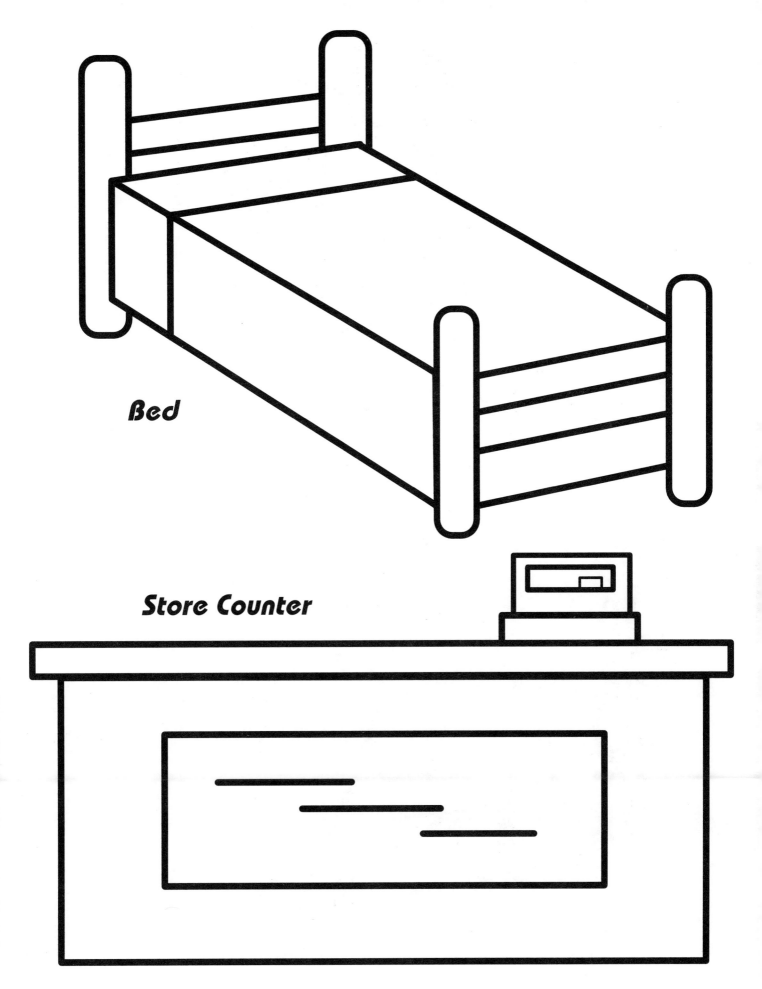

Bed

Store Counter

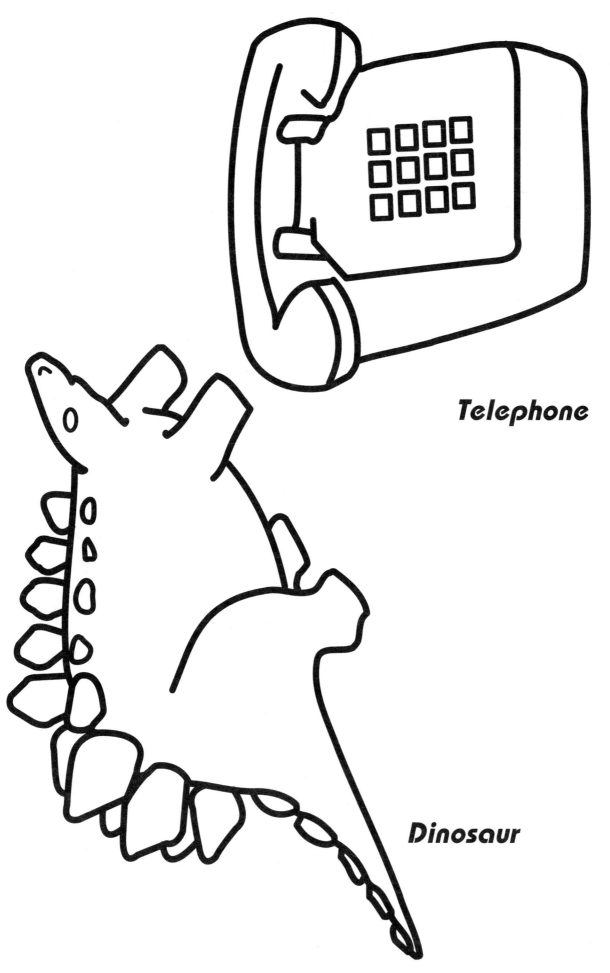

Telephone

Dinosaur

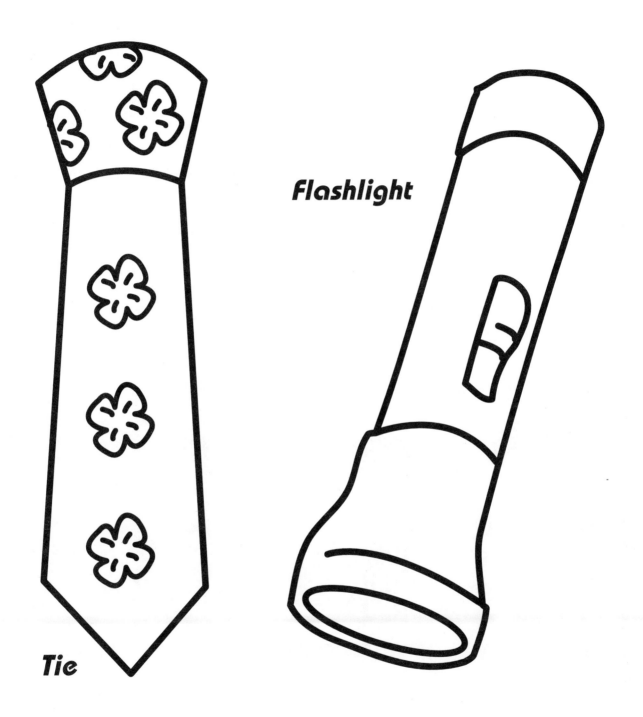

Flashlight

Tie

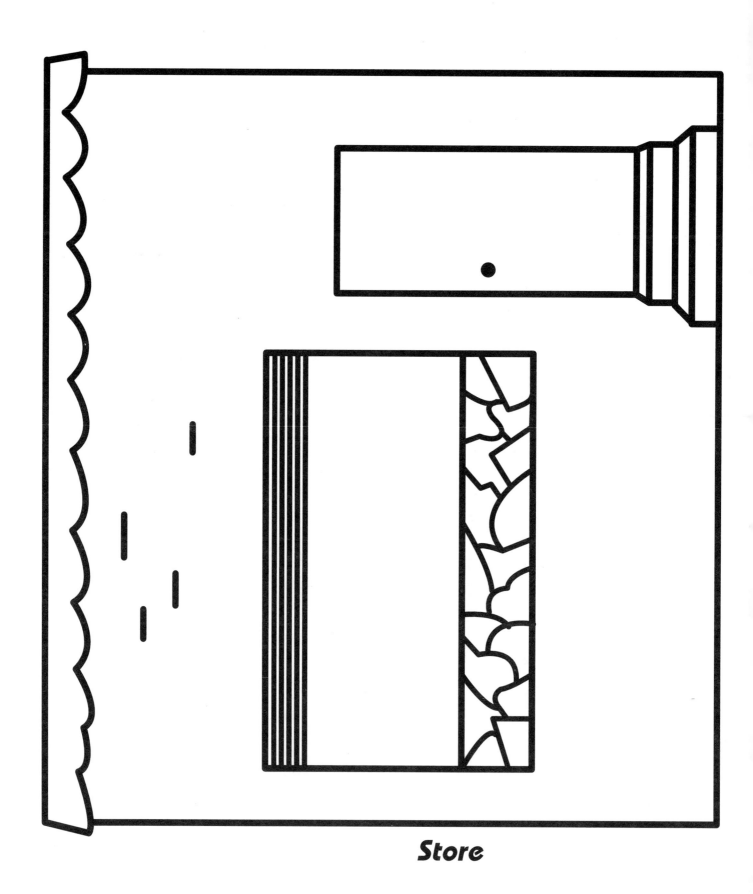

Store

Christmas Tree

Danny Dinosaur

This is a fun story that can be acted out. More children can be added to the story by using patterns from elsewhere in the book.

Pictures needed for the story:

Danny Dinosaur	Evan
Darla Dinosaur	Ellie
Maxwell	school bus
elephant	baseball, bat & glove
house	

One Saturday morning all the **boys** and **girls** were in the park waiting for Danny Dinosaur to come and play baseball with them. He was great at catching high fly balls. To make the game fair, Danny swtched back and forth, playing in the outfield for both teams.

Danny Dinosaur was a Stegosaurus. He was very big. He was as long as a **school bus**, and as high as a **house**. He had a very small head and a very long tail that he used to protect himself. Danny was as heavy as an **elephant**, and on top of his back were plates or fins that looked fierce. Despite Danny's size, he was just a shy gentle animal who liked to eat plants.

The children had been really frightened of Danny at first, but they soon learned he was lonely and wanted to be their friend. They played together every Saturday.

On this particular Saturday, the children didn't hear the *rumble, rumble, shake, shake*, that always preceded Danny's arrival. They waited and waited, but Danny didn't come.

"Something must be wrong with him," said **Evan**.

"We'd better go to his home and find out," said **Ellie**.

Danny Dinosaur lived in the big valley over the hill just outside of town. The boys and girls told their parents where they were going and started out. They walked a long time, and all of a sudden they heard a loud noise. *Oh-oh*, it kept getting louder.

"That sounds like Danny," cried **Maxwell**. "He sounds like he's laughing."

"Let's hurry and find out what's going on," yelled **Evan**.

The noise grew louder as they got closer.

"Look," they all yelled at once. "There are *two* **dinosaurs**." As the **children** approached, **Danny** and his friend stopped laughing and slowly walked toward the children.

"This is my new friend, **Darla**. We were having so much fun I forgot to come to the ball game. I'm sorry," explained Danny.

The boys and girls were so relieved to find that Danny was okay that they started laughing and jumping up and down and clapping their hands.

"Now Danny won't have to play ball on both teams anymore," said Evan. "Darla can play on one team, and Danny can play on the other. We'll be more equally matched."

"Let's go play ball in the park," said **Danny**.

Now there were twice as many rumbles and shakes as the children rode along on Danny and Darla's tails all the way back to the park to **play ball**.

Danny Dinosaur

Darla Dinosaur

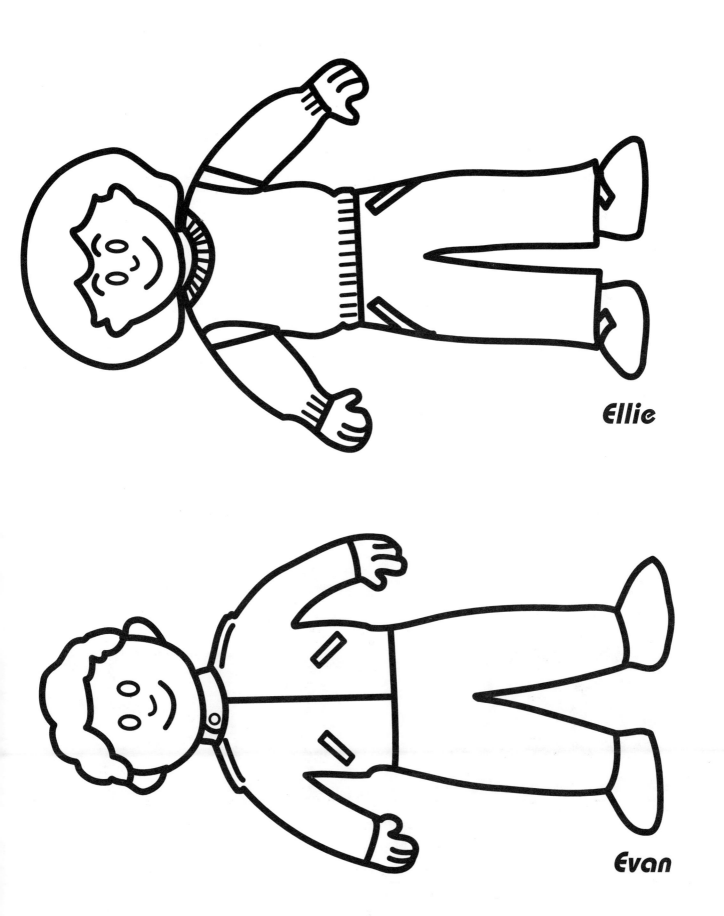

Ellie

Evan

63

House

Maxwell

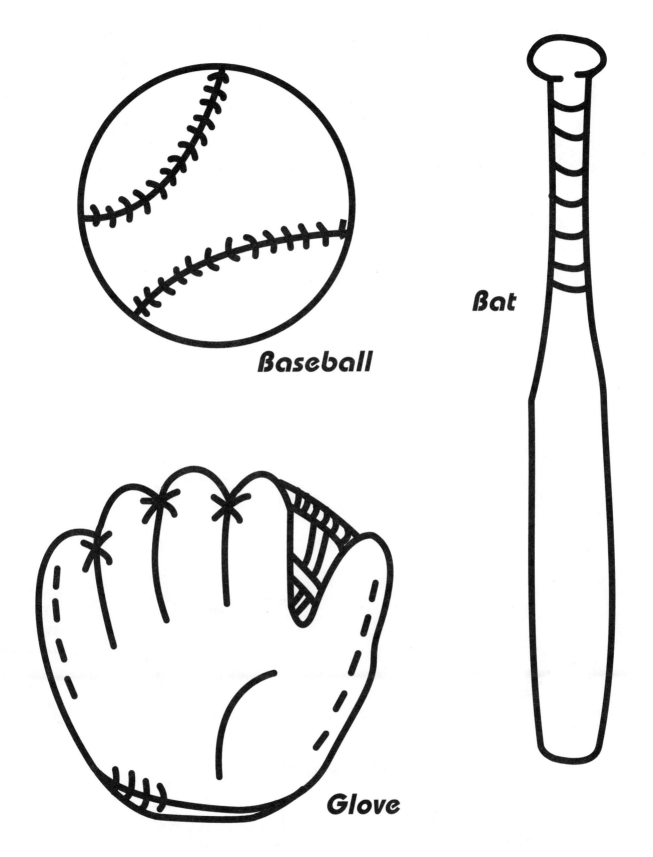

Baseball

Bat

Glove

Bus

Elephant

7 Winter Snow

This story teaches about winter snow. It tells about winter sports and fun activities. The story teaches about birds, their colors and the food they like. It can be acted out or used with the flannelboard.

Pictures needed for this story:

trees	red seeds
house with snow	sunflower seeds
children playing in snow	goldfinch
snowman	bread
sled	apple
ice skates	peanut butter
blue jay	pine cone
cardinal	popcorn
sparrow	

It had been snowing all day. It was a regular blizzard. The roofs of the **houses** were covered with snow. The ground was covered with snow. The **trees** were covered with snow.

The **children** loved the snow. They had on their snow suits, boots, mittens, and hats, and they were keeping warm. **Caleb** was making a **snowman**. **Hannah** and **Timmy** were **sledding**. **Andrew** was skating on a small patch of ice. The children were laughing happily.

But the **birds** were not happy at all. They were hungry. Before the north wind blew the snow into big drifts, the birds had been able to push snow off the meadow grasses and find red sumac and sunflower seeds on the tall stems. The birds could eat the little blue juniper berries high up in the juniper trees. Now everything was covered in the deep snow. All their food was hidden. There was nothing left for them to eat.

The **blue jay** was squawking loudly, looking for food. It liked the **red sumac seeds**, but they were covered with snow. The **red cardinal** was looking for **sunflower seeds** on the tall stems in the garden, but they were covered with snow. The **goldfinch** and the **sparrow** were looking for **bugs** in the bark of the trees, but the trees were covered with snow.

The children saw the birds fluttering around.

"The birds need our help," said **Caleb**.

"Let's get some food for them," said **Hannah**.

"Come in the house and we'll find something for the birds to eat," said **Andrew**.

All the children ran through the deep snow into the house. Caleb found bread and made **bread crumbs**. Andrew found an **apple** and cut it into pieces (with his mother's help). **Hannah** put **peanut butter** all around a **pine cone**, and Timmy made **popcorn**.

"We also have some **sunflower seeds** from the garden," exclaimed Hannah. "I'll roll one **pine cone** in sunflower seeds and one pine cone in popcorn. The peanut butter will help it stick."

When the children had gathered the food, they bundled up again and took it outside.

Hannah tied a string to the **pine cones** and tied them to the **tree branches**. The **cardinal** flew over and started to eat.

Caleb sprinkled **bread crumbs** on top of the snow. The **sparrows** flew over to eat. **Andrew** put the pieces of **apple** on the flat **evergreen** branches and the **blue jays** settled on the branches to eat them.

Timmy put some dishes of **popcorn** on the ground under the **evergreen tree**, and the **goldfinch** flew over and started to eat.

All the birds were eating and chirping happily.

"We will feed the birds everyday as long as their food is covered with snow," said all the **children** together. And they did.

Caleb

Timmy

Hannah

Andrew

Bread

Blue Jay

Sparrow

Cardinal

Snowman

Popcorn

Apple

PEANUT
BUTTER

Peanut butter

Goldfinch

72

House

Pine cone

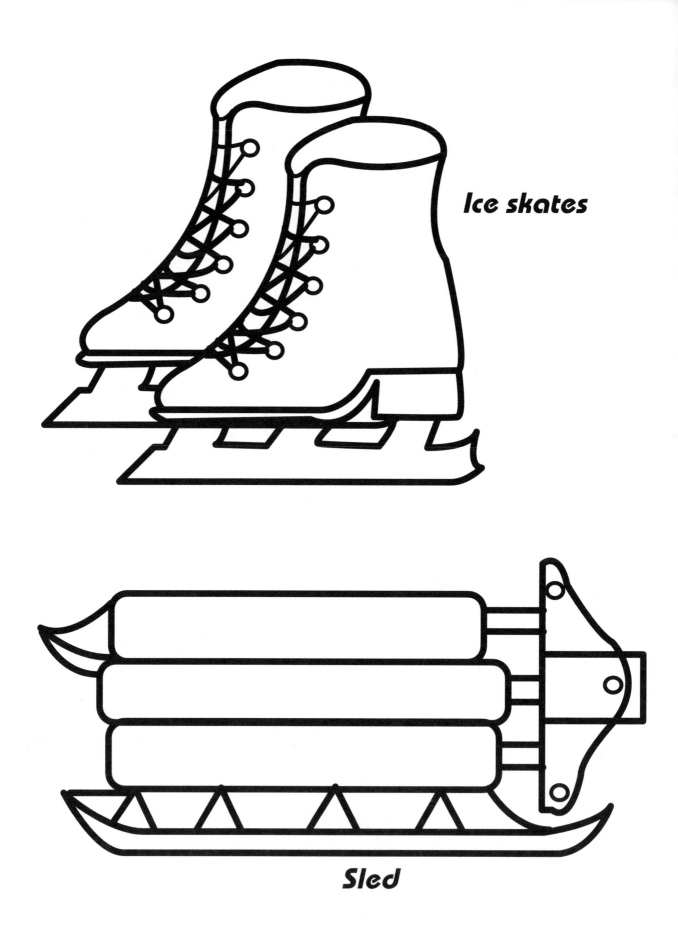

Ice skates

Sled

74

Pine tree

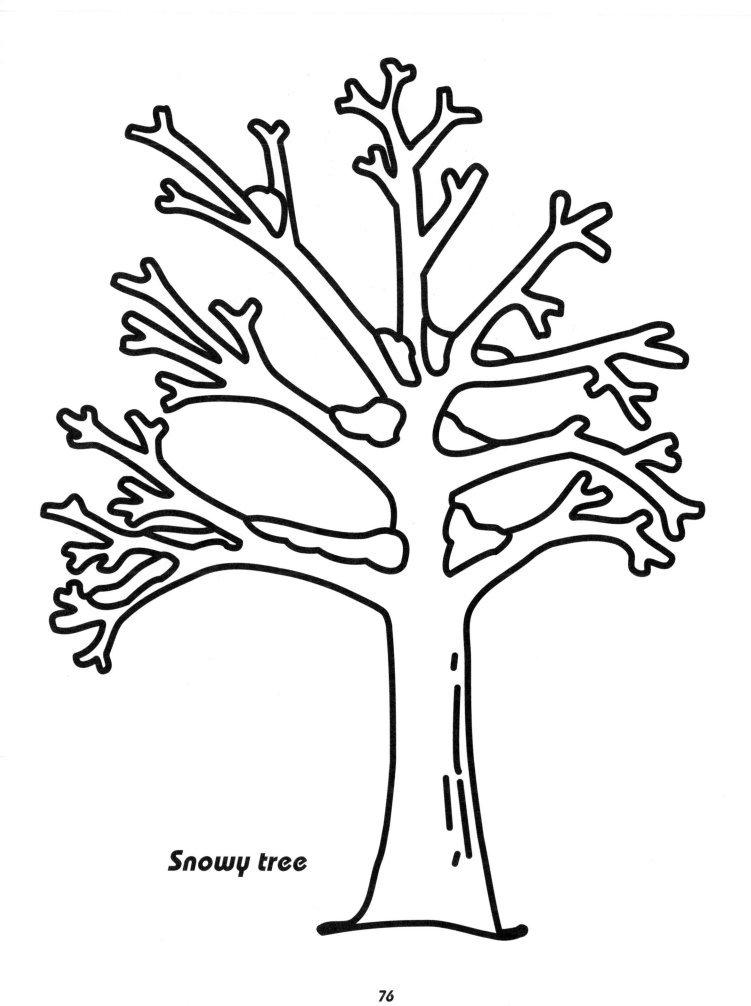

Snowy tree

Sunflower seeds

Red seeds

8 *What Noise Is That?*

This is a story about noises made by different animals while they are eating. It tells what the animals like to eat. Other sounds may be added.

Pictures needed for this story:

horse & apple	fish
sparrow & corn	fish food
fawn & pear	fish bowl
cow & grass	dog & bone
squirrel & walnut	boy & cake
cat & milk	

"*Chomp, chomp,*" goes **Harry Horse** as he eats a chunk out of the **apple**.

"*Peck, peck,*" goes **Sally Sparrow** as she eats a piece of **corn**.

"*Crunch, crunch,*" goes **Fanny Fawn** as she eats the nice **juicy pear**.

"*Mush, mush,*" goes **Clara Cow** as she eats sweet **grass**.

"*Crack, crack,*" goes **Sammy Squirrel** as he eats a big **walnut**.

"*Slurp, slurp,*" goes **Kitty Cat** as she drinks her **milk**.

"*Glub, glub,*" goes **Franny Fish** as she eats her **fish food**.

"*Scrunch, scrunch,*" goes **Dobby Dog** as he eats a **bone**.

"*Yum, yum,*" goes **Billy Boy** as he eats a slice of **cake**.

Chomp, peck, crunch, mush, crack, slurp, glub, scrunch, and *yum* are some eating noises. What noise do you make when you eat?

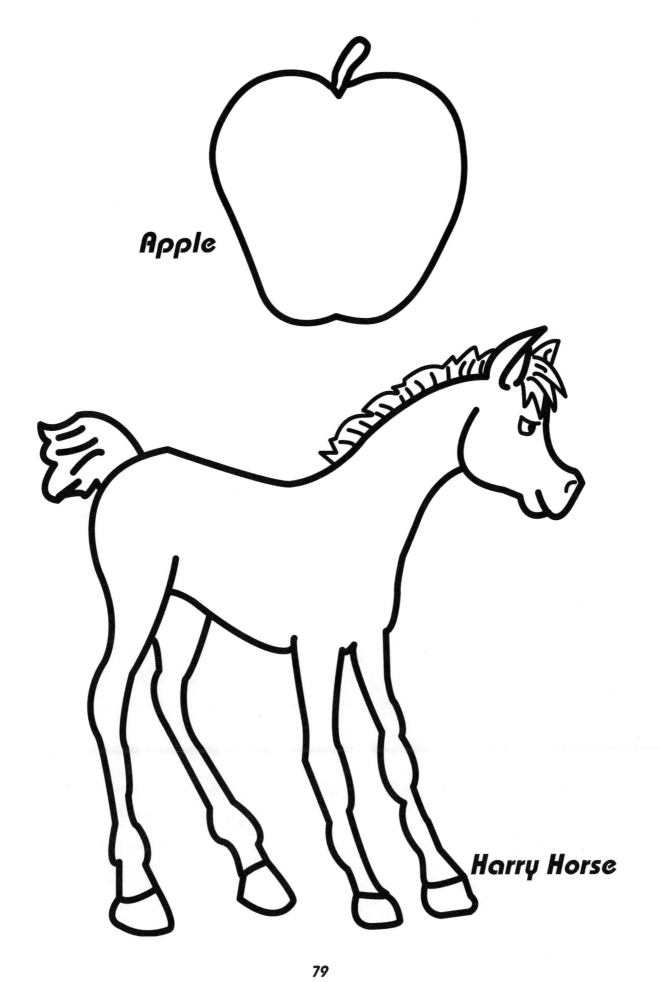

Apple

Harry Horse

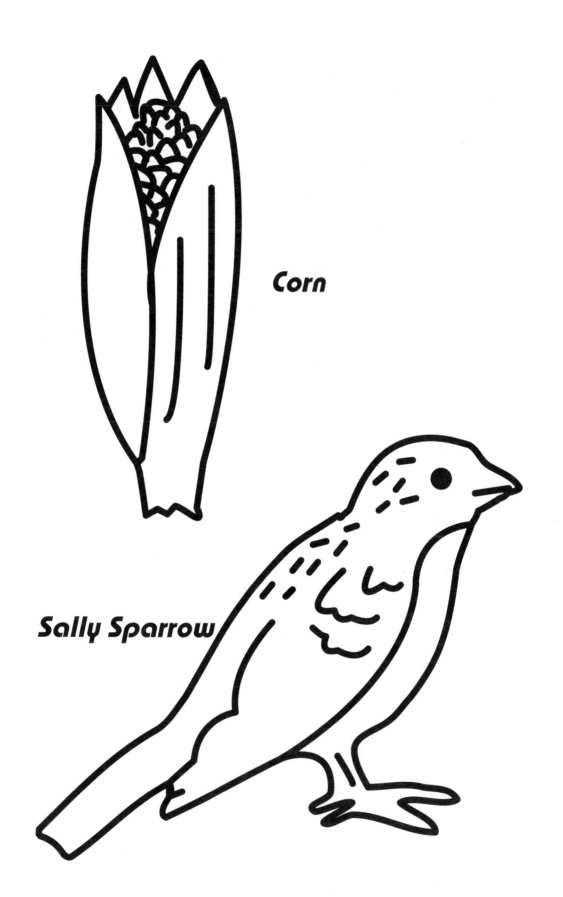

Corn

Sally Sparrow

Fanny Fawn

Pear

Clara Cow

Grass

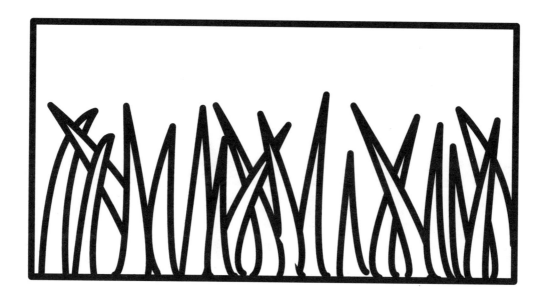

Sammy Squirrel

Walnut

Kitty Cat

Milk

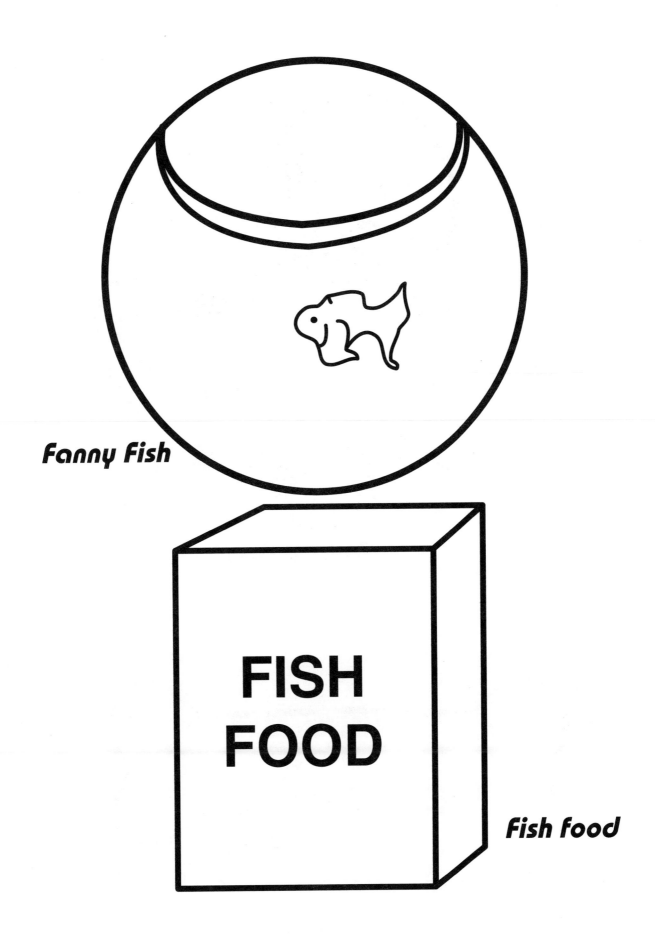

Fanny Fish

FISH FOOD

Fish food

Dobby Dog

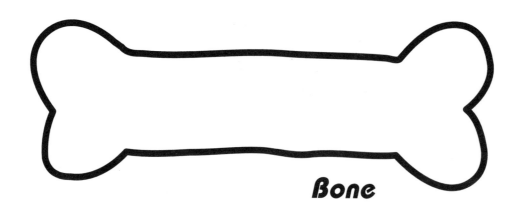

Bone

Cake

Billy

9 Fun at the Zoo

This story tells about some zoo animals. It can be acted out.

Pictures needed for this story:

Claire	rabbit (make several)
Mother	polar bear (make two)
elephant	seal
tiger	monkey (make several, also see p. 107 for another monkey pattern.)
cage	

Claire woke up one morning, jumped out of bed and said, "**Mom**, I want to go to the zoo."

Her mother thought a minute, then said, "All right."

Claire was only five years old so her mother helped her get dressed. After getting ready, they left for the **zoo**.

Claire noticed right away that lots of the animals were in cages. The first animal they saw was the **elephant**. It was throwing straw on its back with its long trunk.

"I like the elephant. It has a long nose," said Claire.

Claire and her mother wandered on a little farther and saw a tiger. The tiger was sleeping.

"I like the **tiger**. It has nice stripes," said Claire.

The monkey cage was just around the corner. The **monkeys** were playing around, swinging by their long arms and tails, having a really good time.

Claire said, "I like the monkeys. They have fun swinging around."

Claire and her mother saw some **rabbits** in the next cage. They were hopping around with their long ears flopping.

"I like the bunny rabbit. It has pretty long ears and a cute fluffy tail," said Claire.

"Oh, let's see if we can find some more animals," said her mother. "I think I hear the **seals** barking. Maybe they are feeding them now."

Sure enough, Claire and her mother watched the seals eat. "I like the way they bark and clap their flippers," Claire laughed.

Next Claire and her mother went to see the **polar bears**."Look, Mom," cried Claire. "They are swimming and playing ball. I like to see them play in the water."

Claire and her **mother** had fun walking around the zoo visiting all the animals.

"Shall we go home now, Claire?" asked her mother. "We'll come back another day and see more animals."

Claire and her mother went home.

Mom

Claire

Elephant

Monkey

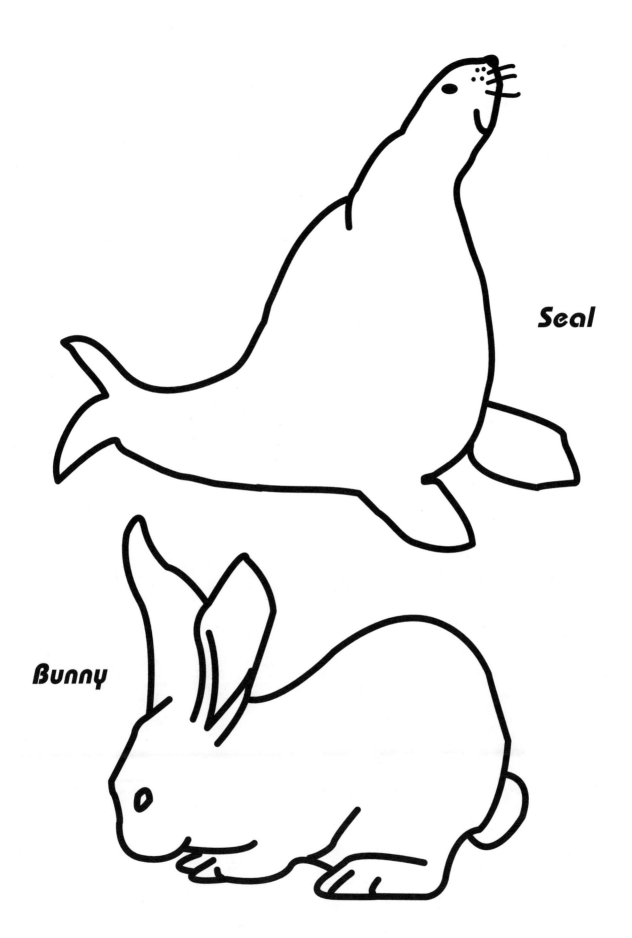

Seal

Bunny

Polar bear

Tiger

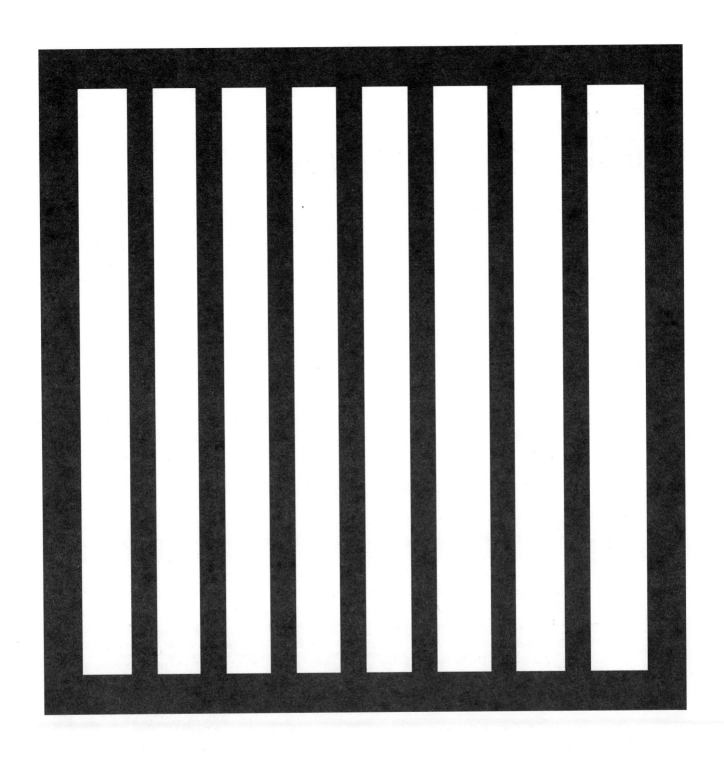

Cage

10 The Little Blue Box

This story teaches some problem-solving skills. Patterns of children can be copied from other stories to create more classmates for this story.

Pictures needed for this story:

Hannah	blue ribbon
mother	several children
scarf	rocks
pin	teacher
earrings	school bags
store	sun
candle	science table
blue egg-shaped candle	desks
blue box	empty blue box

Hannah lived close to school, so she could walk there. She was in kindergarten.

One Saturday, **Hannah** said, "**Mother**, I need to get my teacher a present because her birthday is on Monday."

"What would you like to get her?" asked Mother.

"Maybe a **scarf**, or a **pin**, or **earrings**, or a **candle**," answered Hannah.

"Those are all good ideas," said Mother. "Let's go to the store and look."

Hannah and her mother went to the **store**. They looked and looked and finally decided on a **blue candle shaped like an egg**.

"My teacher will like this," exclaimed Hannah.

Hannah and her mother put the **blue candle** in a **tiny blue box** and wrapped it with **pretty blue paper**. They put a tiny **blue ribbon** on the package.

"Blue is my teacher's favorite color," said Hannah.

On Monday morning, **Hannah** put the teacher's **gift** in her **school bag** and started to walk to school. Several of her **friends** walked with her.

"Let's find some pretty **stones** for our science table," said **Tim**.

The boys and girls put down their school bags and looked for stones in the path.

"I've found **four stones** already," said **Hannah**.

As Hannah picked up her bag she didn't notice that the **teacher's gift** had fallen out and landed in a sunny spot beside the path.

Hannah and her friends walked on to school laughing and singing happily. At school the children put their stones on the **science table**, hung up their school bags and sat down at their **desks**. The children worked hard all morning on their lessons.

Back on the path, the warm **sun shone** on that little **blue box** and kept it warm—very warm.

At lunch time, **Hannah** and her **classmates** decided to sing "Happy Birthday" to their teacher and give her their gifts. When Hannah went to get her gift out of her **school bag**, it was gone.

"Oh my," cried Hannah. "My little blue box is gone. I must have lost it on the path. May I run back and see if I can find it?" she asked the **teacher**.

Hannah's teacher could see that Hannah was very upset so she gave her permission to go back and find the gift.

Hannah quickly ran down the path and looked and looked until she found the little **blue box**. It felt very warm. It had been laying in the sun all morning. Hannah picked it up and ran all the way back to school.

The **teacher** looked at the little blue box and said it was very pretty. She gently unwrapped the gift and opened the box. It was **empty**!

"What happened to the blue candle?" exclaimed **Hannah**.

"I think maybe the sun melted it," explained the teacher, "but I can really use this little **blue box** for my desk."

This made **Hannah** happy.

When Hannah got home after school, she told her mother all about the disappearing candle in the little blue box.

Mother

Hannah

Friends

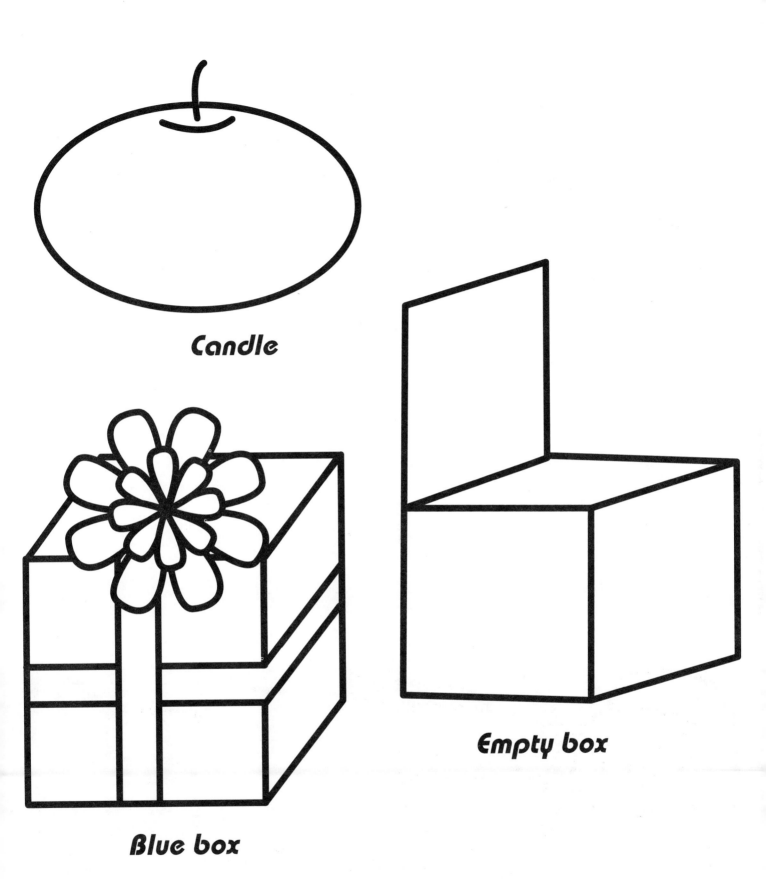

Candle

Blue box

Empty box

Table

Teacher

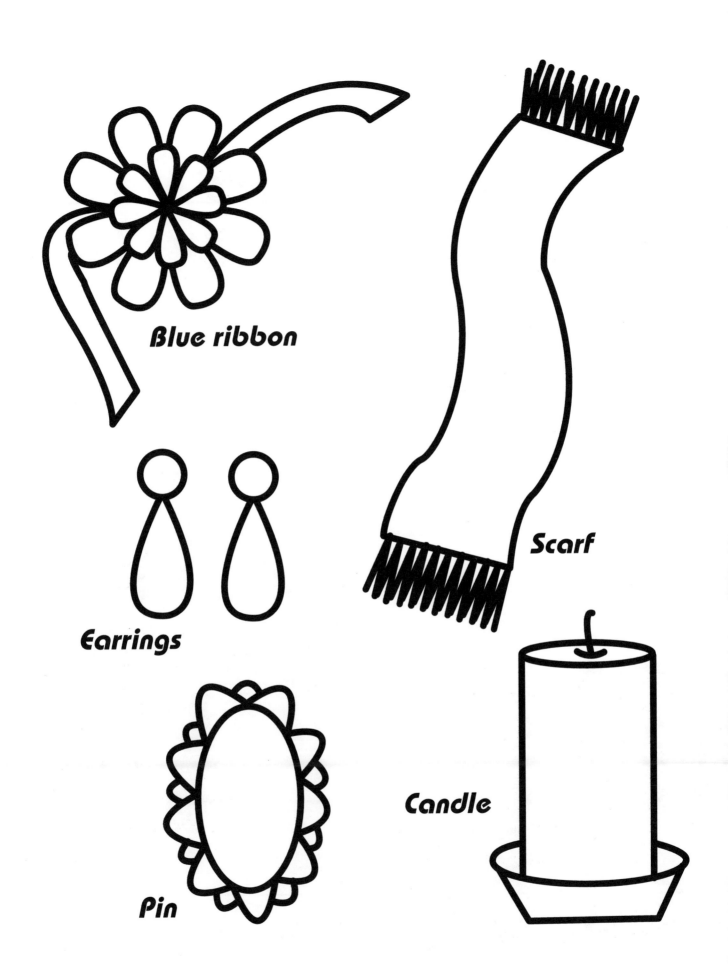

Blue ribbon

Earrings

Pin

Scarf

Candle

Sun

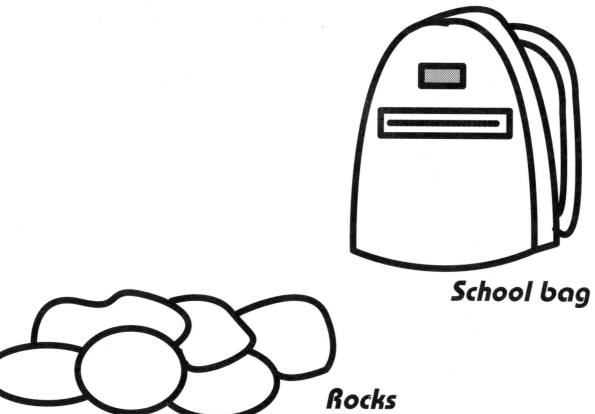

School bag

Rocks

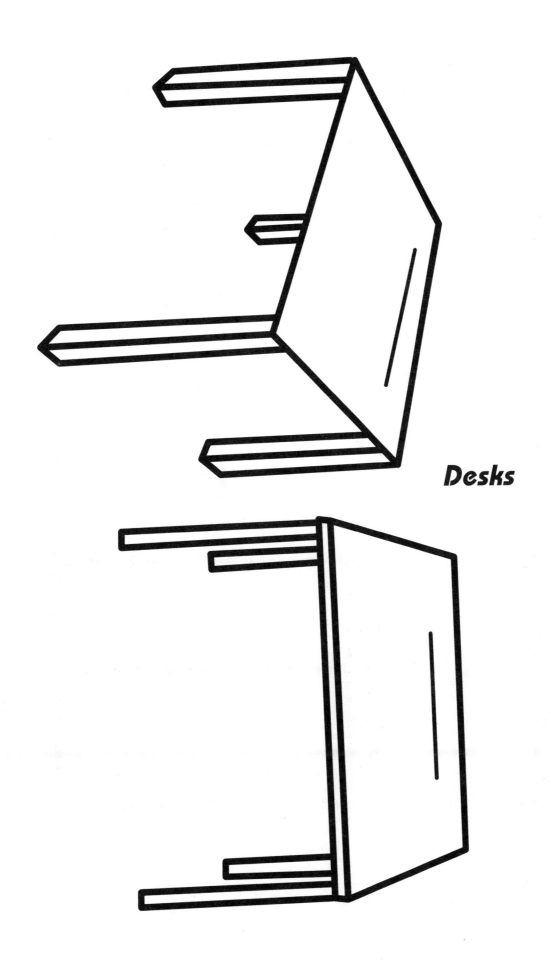

Desks

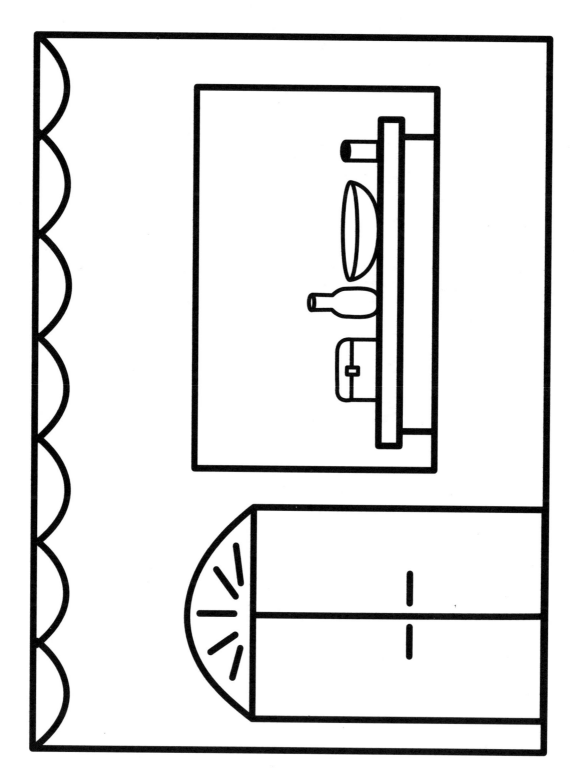

Store

11 Lost Calico Cat

This story tells of different movements and what animals make them. Some problem solving is included and some rhyming poetry is used.

Pictures needed:

girl	bird
snake	stairs
calico cat	bunny
bed	garage
monkey	car
bookcase	house
chair	mouse

Where, oh where, can she be? **My** favorite **stuffed calico cat** had disappeared, just like that.

 I crawled on my **tummy** like a **snake** to look under my **bed**, but my calico cat wasn't there, I said.

 I climbed up on a **chair** like a **monkey** to look on top of my **bookcase**, but I didn't see my calico cat's happy face.

 Where, oh where, can she be? I flew down the **stairs** like a **bird** to look in the hall, but calico cat wasn't there at all.

 I hopped around like a **bunny** to look in the **garage**, near and far, but calico cat wasn't even hiding in the **car**.

 Where, oh where, can she be?

 Then I ran outside of the **house**, where I found my **calico cat** playing hide and seek with a **mouse**.

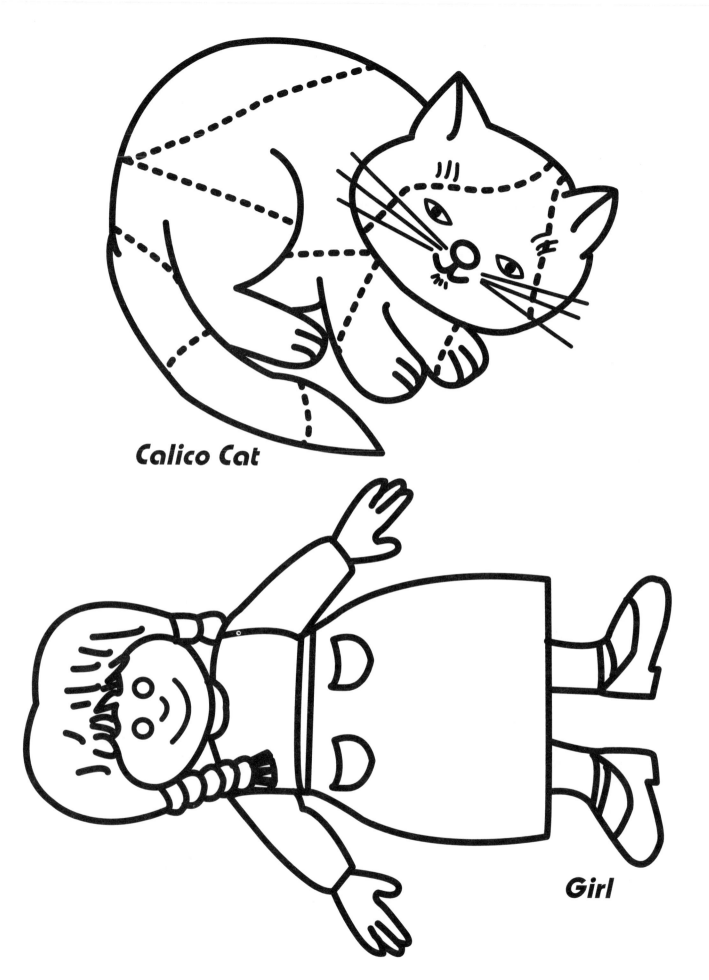

Calico Cat

Girl

Bunny

Bird

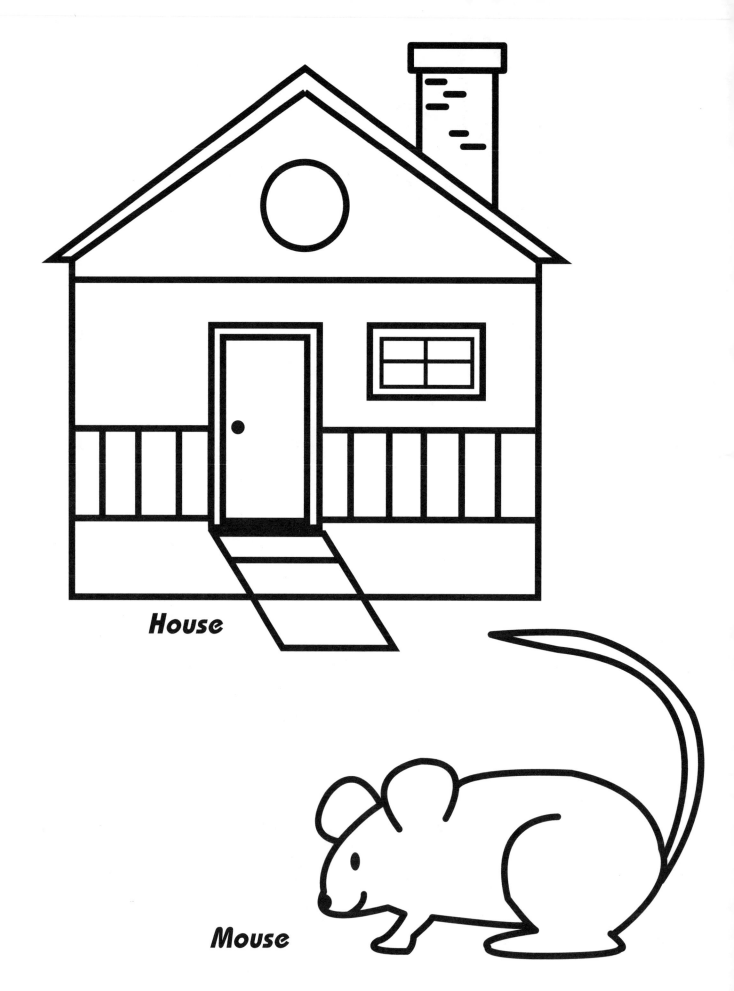

House

Mouse

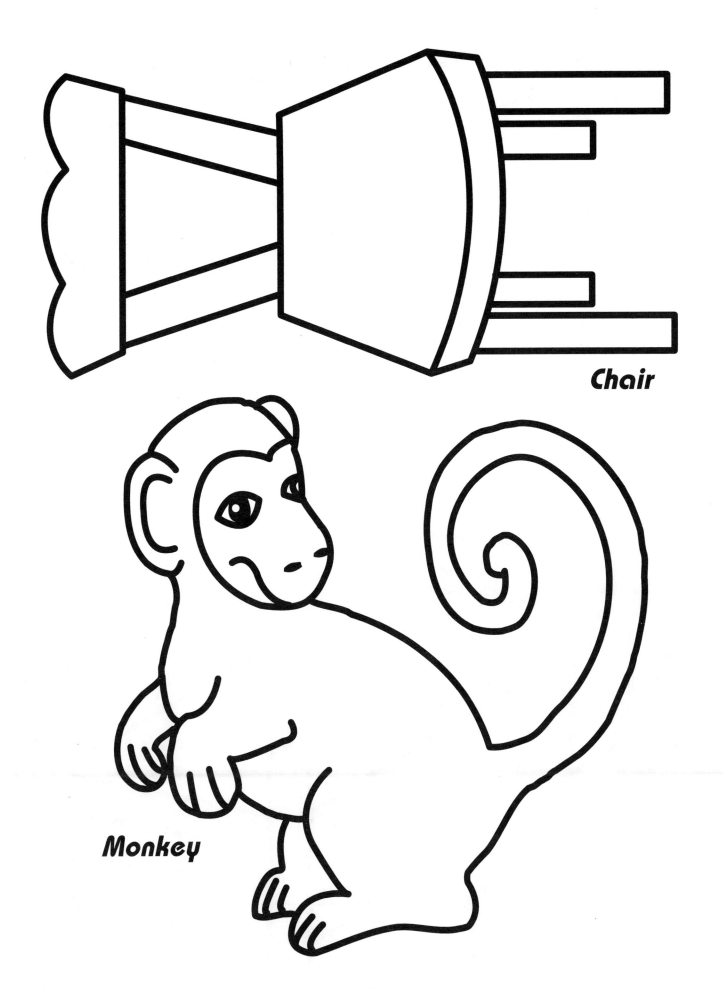

Chair

Monkey

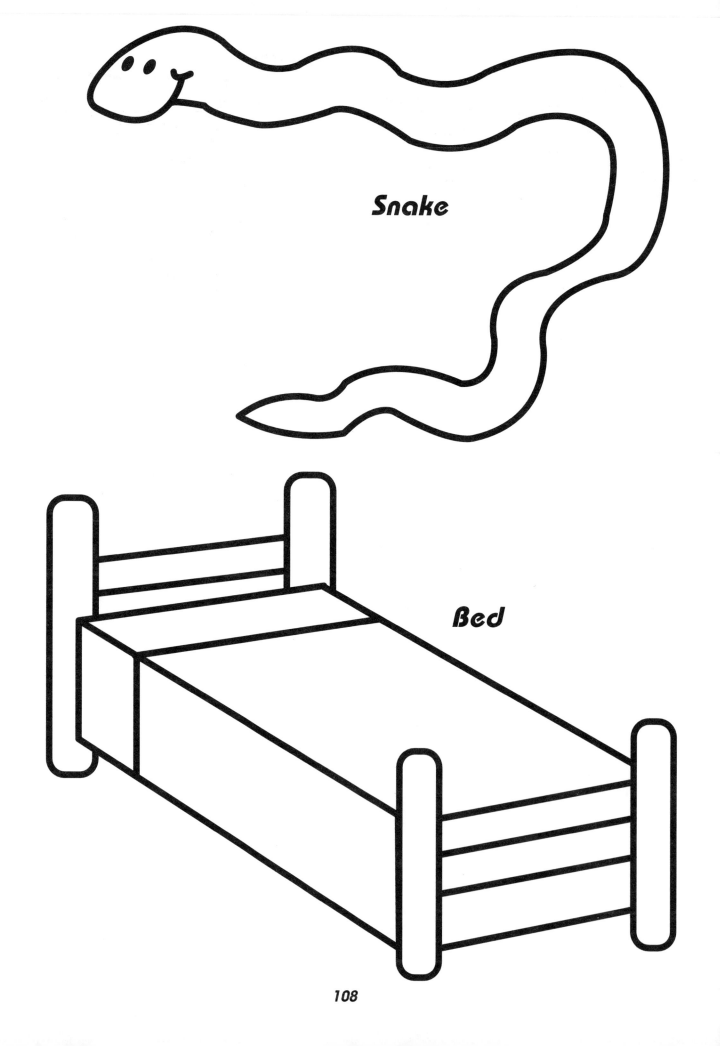

Snake

Bed

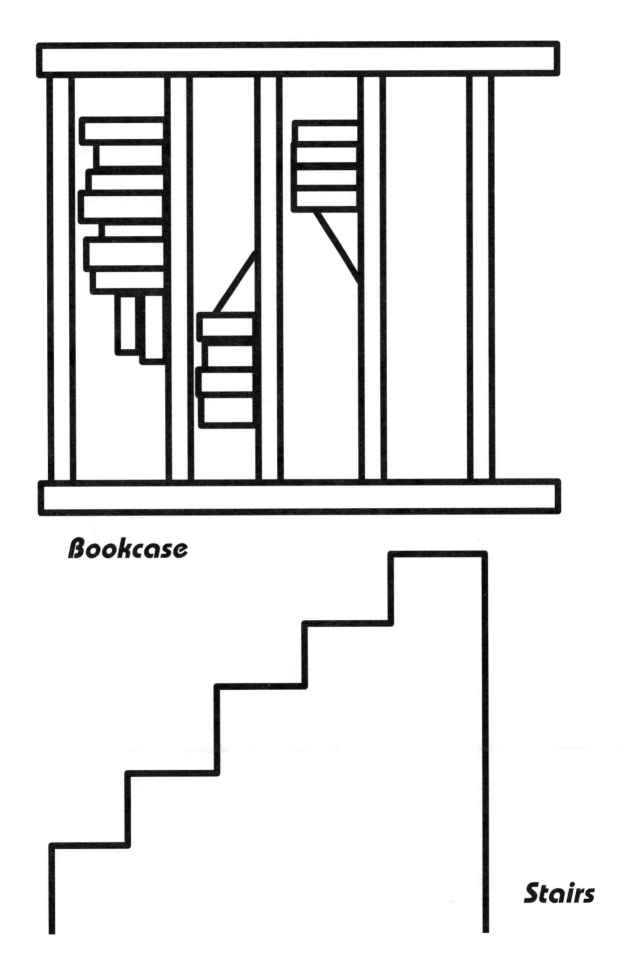

Bookcase

Stairs

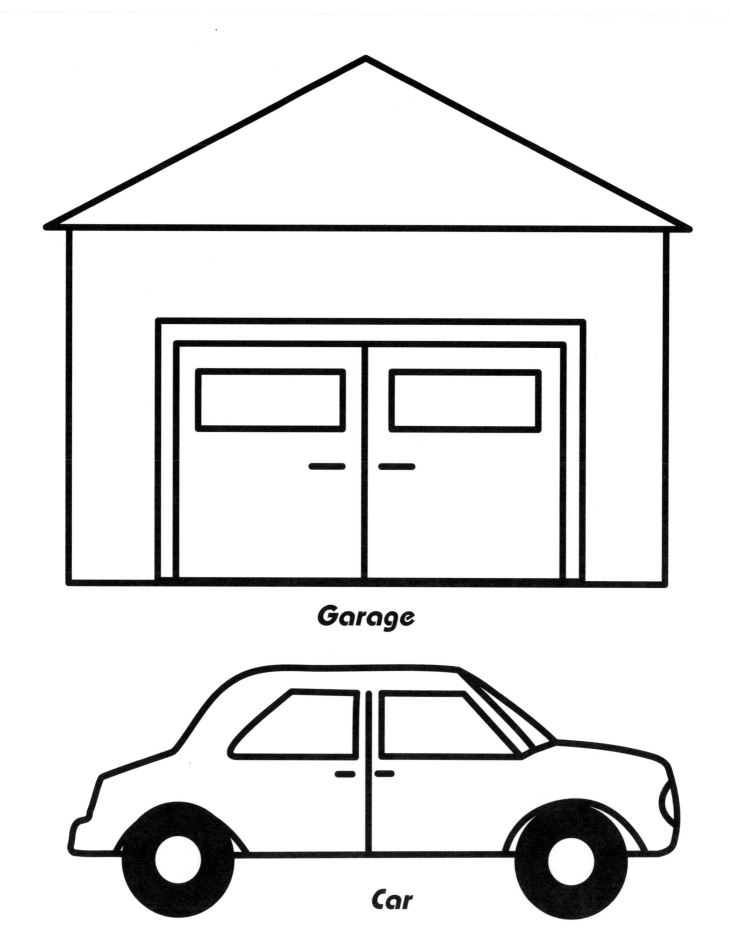

Garage

Car

12 Curtis Squirrel Goes "Nuts"

This story teaches about squirrels and their habits. It has a rhyming song the children will love to sing as they tell the story.

Pictures needed for the story:

squirrels (make several)
trees
maple leaves (orange)
nuts & acorns (big & little; green & brown)
bushes
logs
house with porch
yellow cat

Curtis Squirrel woke up one October morning and said, "I need to start gathering nuts for the winter."

Everyone knows that squirrels love **nuts**. They like **big nuts**, **little nuts**, **green nuts**, **brown nuts**, every kind of nut. Curtis Squirrel was "nuts" about nuts.

Summer was over. This was autumn, and winter would come soon. In winter the ground would be covered with snow, and it was hard to find nuts under the snow.

Curtis Squirrel lived in the hollow of a big **maple tree**. The **leaves** of the maple tree were a beautiful orange color and were beginning to fall to the ground. Many of Curtis Squirrel's **friends** were also gathering nuts for the winter.

"Hi, Curtis," called **Sally** Squirrel from under the **oak tree** where she was looking for **acorns** to eat.

All the squirrels were scampering about busily going from tree to tree, filling their cheeks with nuts and then taking them to their nests.

Curtis Squirrel and his friends were chattering and singing as they worked, "Chatter, chatter, scatter, scatter, up and down, it doesn't matter. All around we will run, finding nuts will be fun."

Sometimes Curtis had his mouth so full of nuts that he just mumbled along.

Curtis Squirrel hid every nut he didn't eat, putting them in many special places. He hid some in **tree trunks**, some in **thick bushes** and many under the **porch steps**.

Every once in a while Curtis would stop to rest. He even went to sleep in an **old log** for awhile. When he woke up, he had to work very hard to catch up with his friends.

"Chatter, chatter, scatter, scatter, up and down, it doesn't matter. All around we will run, finding nuts will be fun." Everyone kept singing this song.

All of a sudden **Curtis** yelled, "Everyone hide, there is a **big yellow cat**."

The squirrels all hid as fast as they could, and waited until the cat was gone.

When the sun went down and it started getting dark, Curtis and the other squirrels went back to their nests to rest. What a busy day it had been.

The days began to get shorter and colder and soon the snow covered the ground. The squirrels were all snug and warm in their nests. They had dried leaves for blankets and plenty to eat.

Once in a while in the winter, when snow covered the ground, **Curtis Squirrel** would wander out of his warm house in the tree, and poke around in the snow looking for more nuts. He even found the nuts he had hidden under the porch. Curtis Squirrel was really "nuts" about nuts.

"Chatter, chatter, scatter, scatter, up and down, it doesn't matter. All around we will run, finding nuts will be fun."

Squirrel

Log

112

Cat

Maple leaves

Acorns & walnuts

Oak tree

House

Bushes

13 Dream Magic

This story teaches about big and little.

Pictures needed for this story:

Faith	big & little stream
Marjorie	big house
mushroom	little house
tea set	

Faith was a very big girl. **Marjorie** was a very tiny girl. Faith lived in a very big house. Marjorie lived in a very tiny house.

One day a strange thing happened. **Faith**, the very big girl, was walking in the garden, and she became thirsty.

"I guess I'll take a drink from the **stream**," she said. "It's nice and cold." As she did so, she started to **become small**.

"What's happening to me? I'm getting smaller and smaller!" exclaimed **Faith**.

Soon she was as small as **Marjorie** the tiny girl.

"What shall I do? I don't belong in this world," cried **Faith**.

Marjorie was sitting on a **mushroom**, and she said, "Hello, I'm **Marjorie**. Who are you?"

"I was a big girl called **Faith**," she cried, "but now I'm tiny like you."

"Oh, oh! You must have taken a drink from the magic stream," said **Marjorie**. "I'm glad, because now I have a new friend."

"I don't want to be your friend. I want to get big again and go home," wailed **Faith**.

"If you'll play with me awhile, I'll tell you the secret of the magic stream," said **Marjorie**.

"Will it make me big again?" asked **Faith**. "If I am tiny when I go home, no one will see me, and someone will step on me."

"Yes, you'll grow big again," said **Marjorie**.

"What will we play?" asked **Faith**.

"Let's play **tea party** under the **mushroom** umbrella. You can be the child and I'll be the mother," said **Marjorie**.

Actually **Faith** had a wonderful time, and she and **Marjorie** became the best of friends.

After awhile **Faith** was tired and getting homesick, and she said, "Can I go home now?"

"All right, if you promise to come back another day," replied **Marjorie**.

"You will have to tell me the secret of the magic stream then," said Faith.

"When you drink the water, it makes you small, and when **you wash your face** in it, you become big," **Marjorie** told her.

Faith washed her face in the **magic stream** and she was soon back to her normal size.

"Wow, what an experience," thought Faith. "Maybe I was just having a dream."

Marjorie

Faith

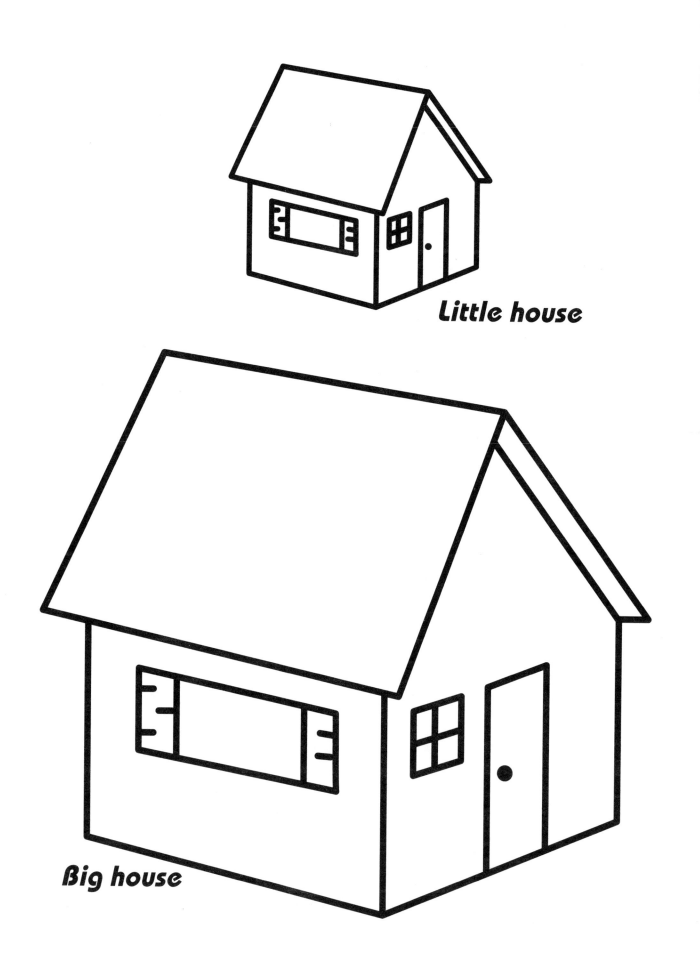

Little house

Big house

120

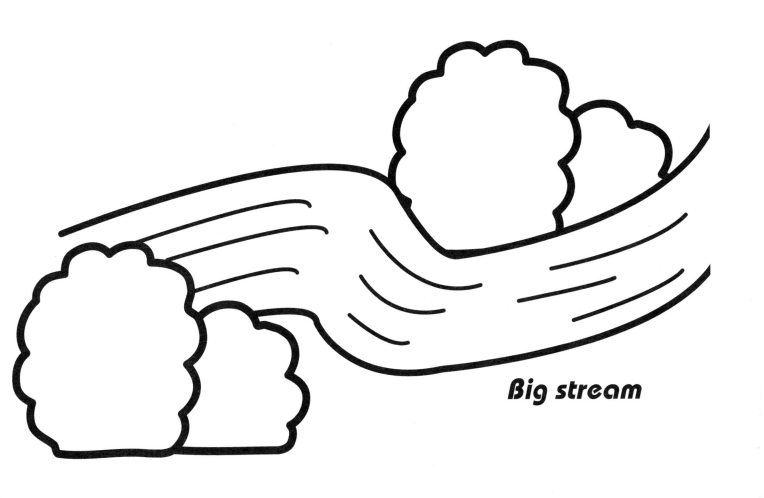

Big stream

Little stream

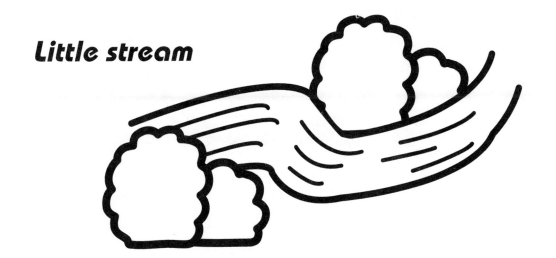

121

Tea set

Mushroom

14 Mixed Up

This story teaches some problem solving and letter and rhyming sounds.

Pictures needed for this story:

Bruce	***cards with words:***
teacher	play - stay
doctor	long - song
Bruce's parents	crowd - loud
children	quiet - diet
	school - pool
	clap - slap
	no - go
	stand - band

Bruce was a cute little boy with red hair and freckles. Bruce had a problem; he was a mixed up kid.

When **I** asked Bruce to come and "**play**" with me, he packed his bags to come and "**stay**" with me.

When *I* asked Bruce if he knew how "**long**" he was, he started to sing a "**song**."

One day things got really weird. When the **teacher** asked Bruce to join the "**crowd**," he thought she said to talk "**loud**." When the teacher told him to be "**quiet**," he thought she said go on a "**diet**."

Something was wrong, very wrong. **Bruce** was doing some very strange things. The **boys** and **girls** in the class decided to find out why Bruce was so mixed up, and they needed to know fast.

"Bruce, we are your **friends**, and we would like to help you in '**school**,'" said **Bill**.

"I think it's too cold to go in the "'**pool**,'" answered **Bruce**.

The boys and girls looked at each other. What is wrong? Can't Bruce hear? They told the **teacher**.

"Let's give Bruce a hearing test," said the teacher.

They said "**clap**." Bruce said "**slap**." They said "**no**;" he said "**go**." They said "**stand**;" he said "**band**."

This little word test solved the mystery. **Bruce** couldn't hear very well. Bruce was hearing the sounds all muddled and not clearly.

The teacher sent a note home to Bruce's **parents** about his hearing difficulty, and they immediately called the **doctor** to have his hearing tested.

The **doctor** "fixed" **Bruce's ears** and solved his hearing problem for years.

Can you think of ways to solve a hearing problem?

Bruce

Doctor

Friends

Bruce's parents

Teacher

PLAY	STAY
LONG	SONG
CROWD	LOUD
QUIET	DIET
SCHOOL	POOL
CLAP	SLAP

STAND	BAND
NO	GO

15 The Five Senses

This story teaches about the five senses; many different items may be used Children from other stories can be used to create classmates for this story.

Pictures needed are:

Jeanne	mouth
teacher	cookies
ear	milk
Curtis	nose
girls	table
eyes	mouse cage
book	hand (fingers)

Jeanne was in kindergarten. She was learning many new things.

The **children** were all gathered around the **teacher**. She was reading a **story** to them. Jeanne was not listening.

"Jeanne, please be quiet and listen to the story," the teacher said.

"I'll have to tell my **ears** to listen," said **Jeanne**.

The teacher was showing the children some beautiful **pictures in the book**.

"Jeanne, please look at the pictures," the teacher said.

"I'll have to tell my **eyes** to look," **Jeanne** said.

It was time for snack so all the children washed their hands and sat at the **tables** for snack. Today they had many different kinds of **cookies** and a cup of **milk**.

"I like the taste of the chocolate cookies," said **Curtis**, "and I like the smell."

"You are using your **mouth** for tasting and your **nose** for smelling," remarked the **teacher**.

"I'm using my mouth to taste, and my nose is working, too," said Jeanne. "I can smell the **mouse cage**."

Everyone said, "Yuck," when Jeanne said that.

"I like the way the different cookies feel," said Jeanne. "The **molasses** cookies feel **smooth** and **soft**. The **chocolate chip cookies** feel **rough** and **hard**."

"You are using your sense of **touch**," explained the teacher. "This morning, boys and girls, we have learned about our five senses. Let's name them."

Jeanne

Curtis

Teacher

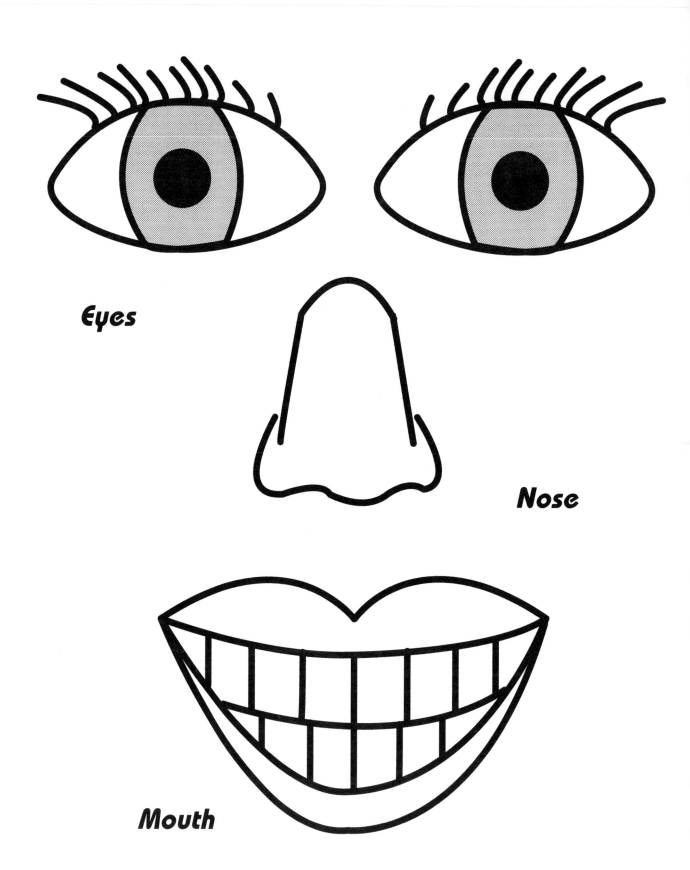

Eyes

Nose

Mouth

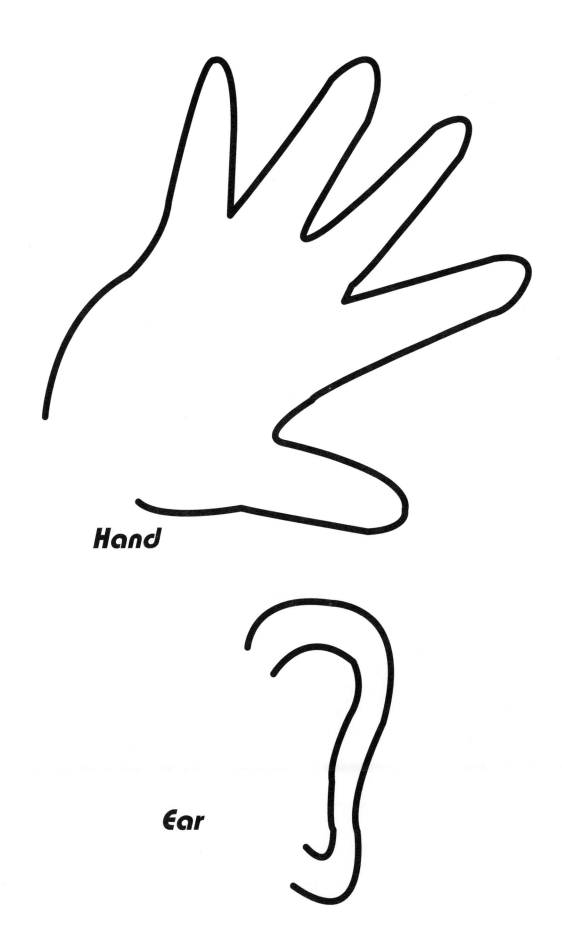

Hand

Ear

Mouse cage

Table

Book

137

Cookies & milk

16 Alice

This story teaches about time, following a schedule, planning ahead and about how family members can help. This story can be acted out. Do you do things in the same sequence as Alice when you get ready for school?

Pictures needed for this story:

Alice	Father
bus	sister
clock	lunchbox
Mother	comb
soap	Grandfather
washcloth	Grandmother
toothbrush	bed
brother	table

Alice was in first grade. She remembered how she had missed the bus the first day of kindergarten. Alice never missed the bus again. To make sure she was on time, she decided to do all the same things to get ready for school each day.

"I set my **clock** for seven o'clock," Alice told her **mother**.

"I put my **clothes** out the night before," Alice told her **father**.

"I'll remember to wash my face and hands with **soap** and a **washcloth**," Alice told her **sister**.

"I'll remember to brush my **teeth** with a **toothbrush** and **toothpaste**," Alice told her **brother**.

"I'll be sure to have my **lunchbox** ready," Alice told her **grandmother**.

"I'll remember to **comb** my hair," Alice told her **grandfather**.

When morning came, Alice was up at seven o'clock. She made her **bed, washed** her face and hands, ate her breakfast, got **dressed**, **combed** her hair, **brushed** her teeth, picked up her **lunchbox** and was all ready when the **bus** came. She got on the bus and went to school.

Alice

Lunchbox

Comb

Brother

Sister

Mother

Father

Grandfather   **Grandmother**

Clock

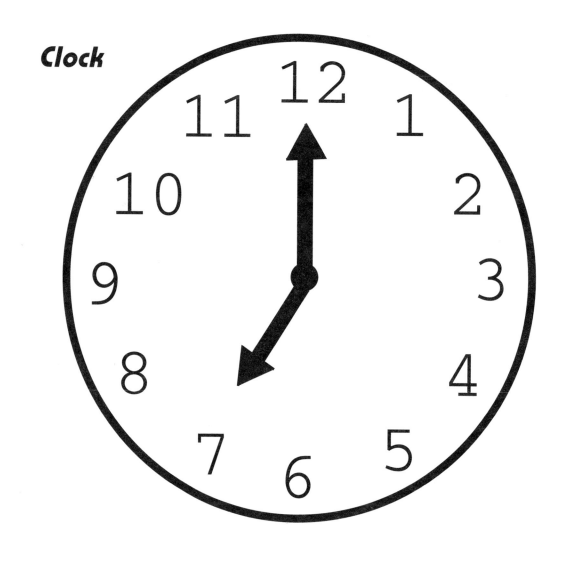

Washcloth

Soap

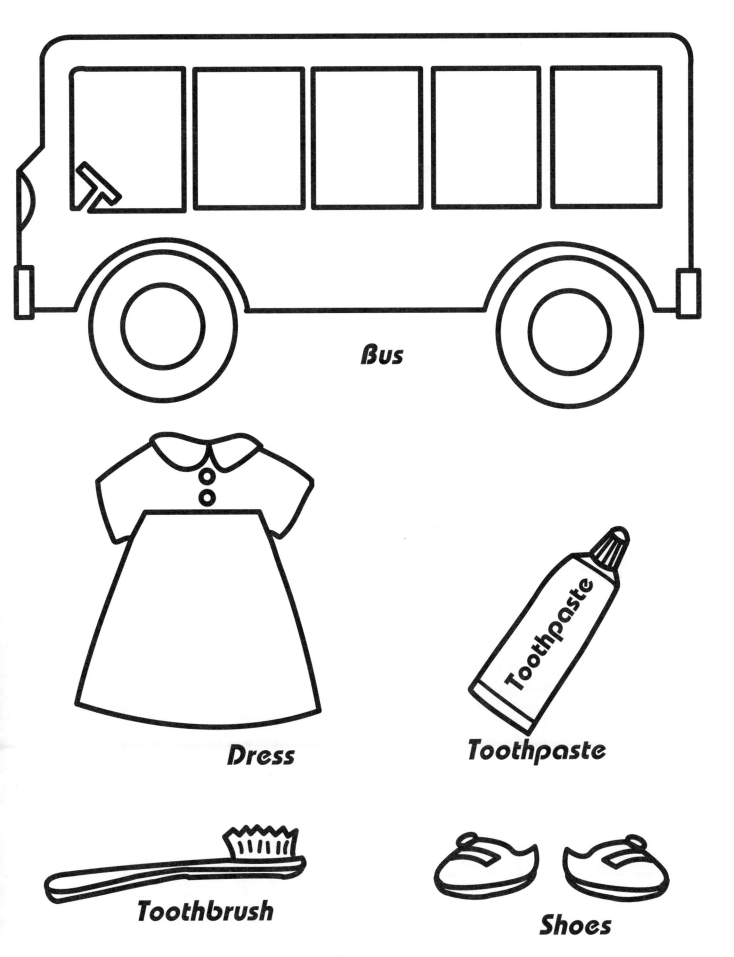

Bus

Dress

Toothpaste

Toothbrush

Shoes

145

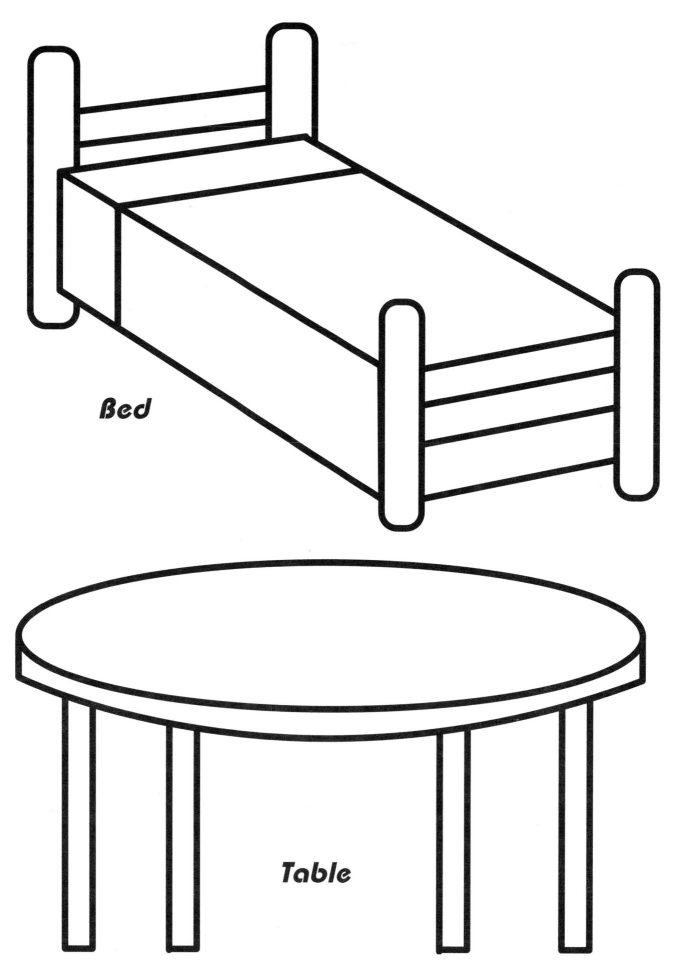

Bed

Table

146

17 *The Middle of the Night*

This story tells about the care of books.

Pictures needed for this story:

Andrew	bookshelf
Mother	rabbit
new teddy bear book	wind
tree	dirty torn book
spider (web)	mended book
owl (feathers)	bed
rain drops	dresser
toy box	blanket

Andrew likes books. He was just learning to read in the second grade. For his birthday Andrew got a new **book** about teddy bears.

"I just love my book, **Mom**," said Andrew. "Will you read my new book to me now?"

Andrew went to get his **book** for his mother to read. "I think I left it in my bedroom," said Andrew.

When Andrew looked in his bedroom, it wasn't there. He looked in the **bookcase**, where books are supposed to be. No book was there. He looked on his **dresser**; he looked in his **toy box**. He even looked under his **bed**. No teddy bear book could be found.

"I can't find my book," **Andrew** told his **mom**.

"You just got your book yesterday, Andrew. Can't you remember where you put it?" asked his mom.

It was getting dark outside and Andrew had to go to bed, so they would have to wait and look for the teddy bear book in the morning.

Outside, in the middle of the night, the new **teddy bear book** was getting all wet. Andrew had left the book out in the **rain**, on a **blanket** under a **tree**.

"Oh dear," the little book cried, "I'm going to be ruined."

Andrew had taken the book outside to read by the big maple tree. It was a nice sunny day—and he wanted to be outside. The problem was, when he had finished looking at the pictures, he had gone off to play and had forgotten it. The **teddy bear book** was left outside all night. In the middle of the night it had started to rain.

A **bunny rabbit** hopped over the book and left its **footprints** on the book in the middle of the night.

The **wind blew** very hard and turned the pages of the book in the middle of the night.

A **spider** started to spin a **web** on the book in the middle of the night, and the rain glistened on the web as it moved in the wind.

An **owl** in the tree above the book started hooting and some **feathers** floated down on the book in the middle of the night.

The little book was really wet. The wind had **torn some pages**. The rabbit **footprints** and the **spider web** and **feathers** had made spots and **dirt on the book**.

The little teddy bear book cried and cried, "I hope Andrew finds me in the morning before anything else happens to me."

The next morning **Andrew** came to breakfast and asked his **mom** if she had found his book.

"No, I haven't seen your book. Can't you think where it might be?" asked his mother.

Andrew thought and thought. Then he said, "Maybe I left it outside. Oh, no, it will be ruined."

He immediately got dressed and ran outside to the **maple tree**. Sure enough, there was his **teddy bear book**. It was all wet and **torn and dirty**. Andrew picked it up and carried it in to show his mother.

"Look, **Mom**, my book is ruined," cried **Andrew**.

"Let me look at it," said his mother.

She inspected the **book**, then she said, "We can save the book this time. But you must remember to treat your books gently and kindly, like a good friend, next time. Come here, Andrew, and you can help me mend your book with 'kindness.'"

The **teddy bear book** never looked new again, but it was mended and cleaned and treated like a good friend after that. **Andrew** learned to always take care of his books and never leave them outside

Mother

Andrew

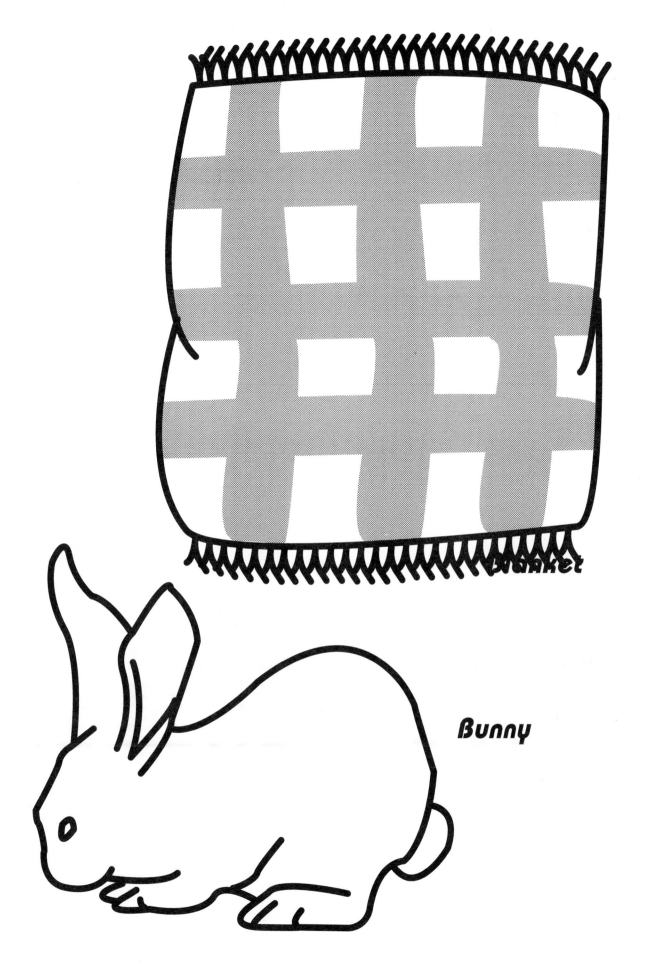

Blanket

Bunny

149

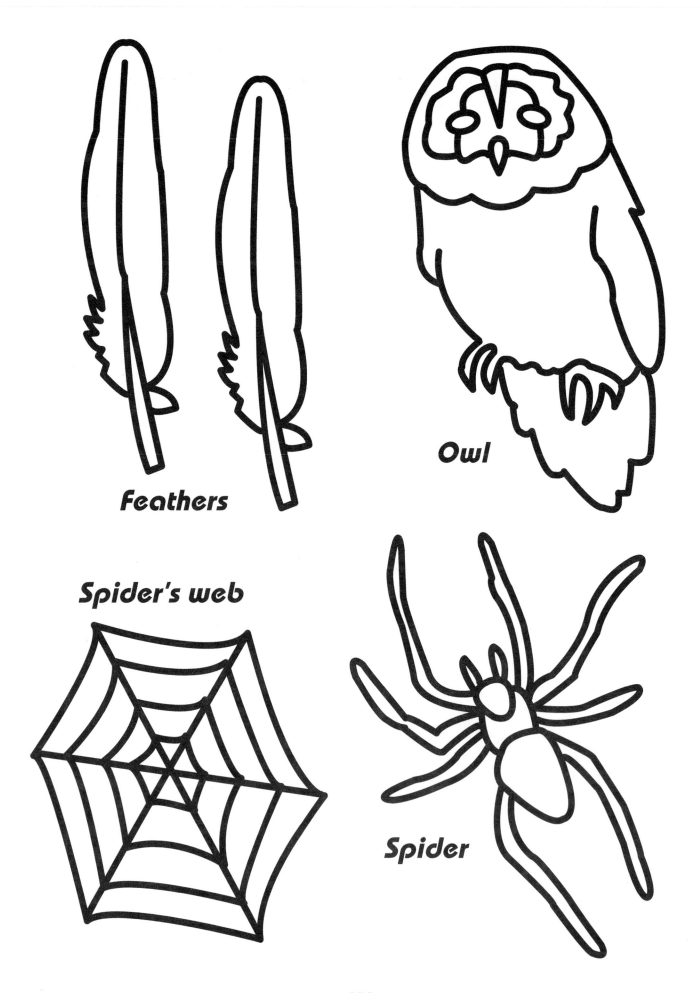

Feathers

Owl

Spider's web

Spider

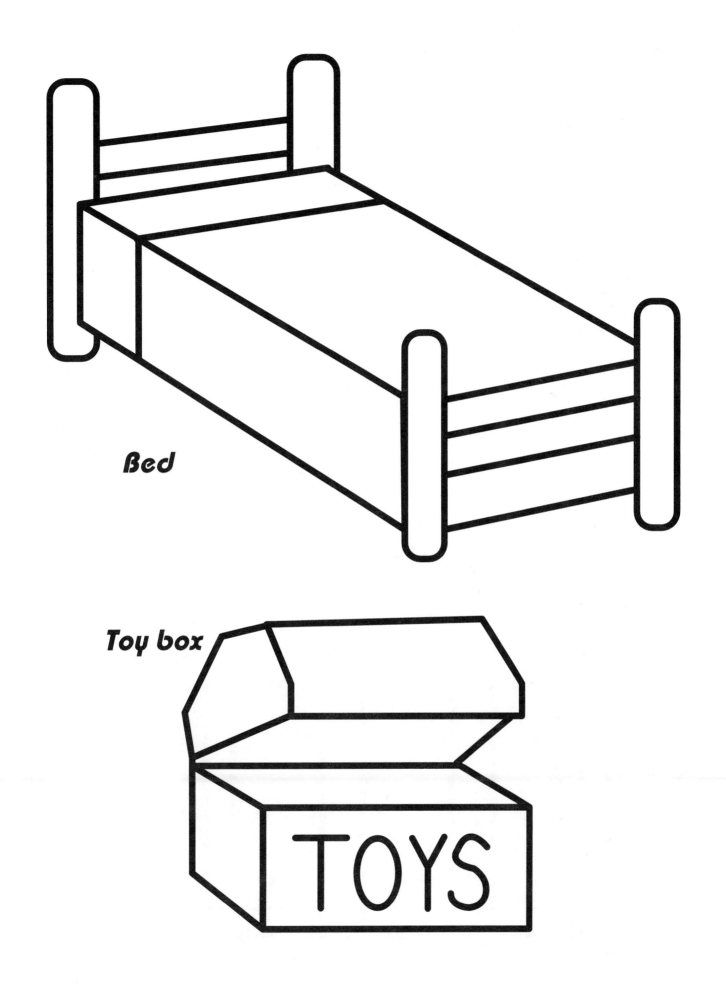

Bed

Toy box

TOYS

151

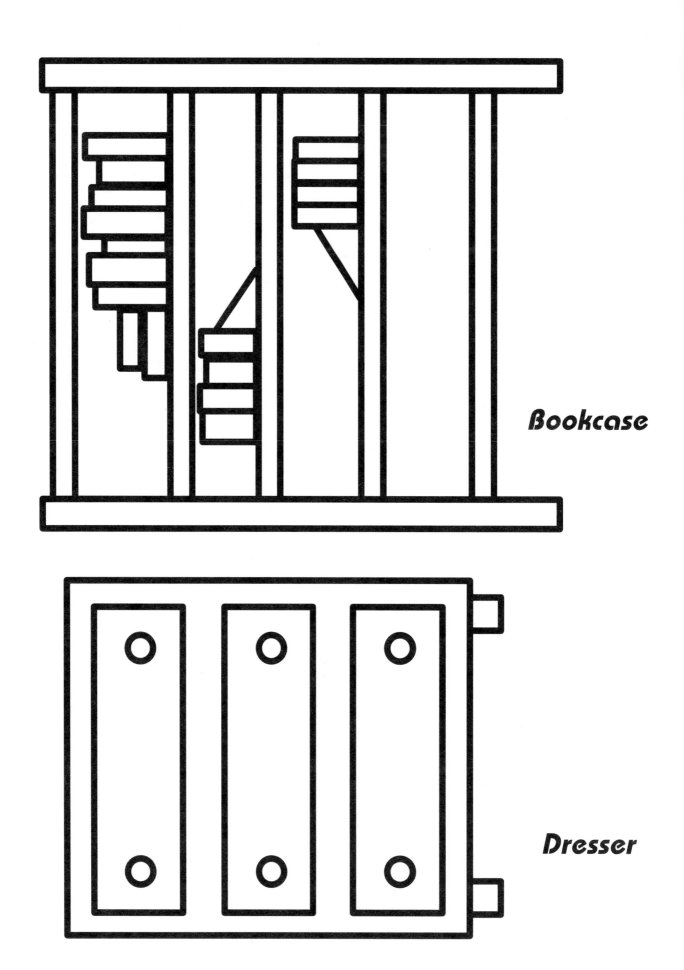

Bookcase

Dresser

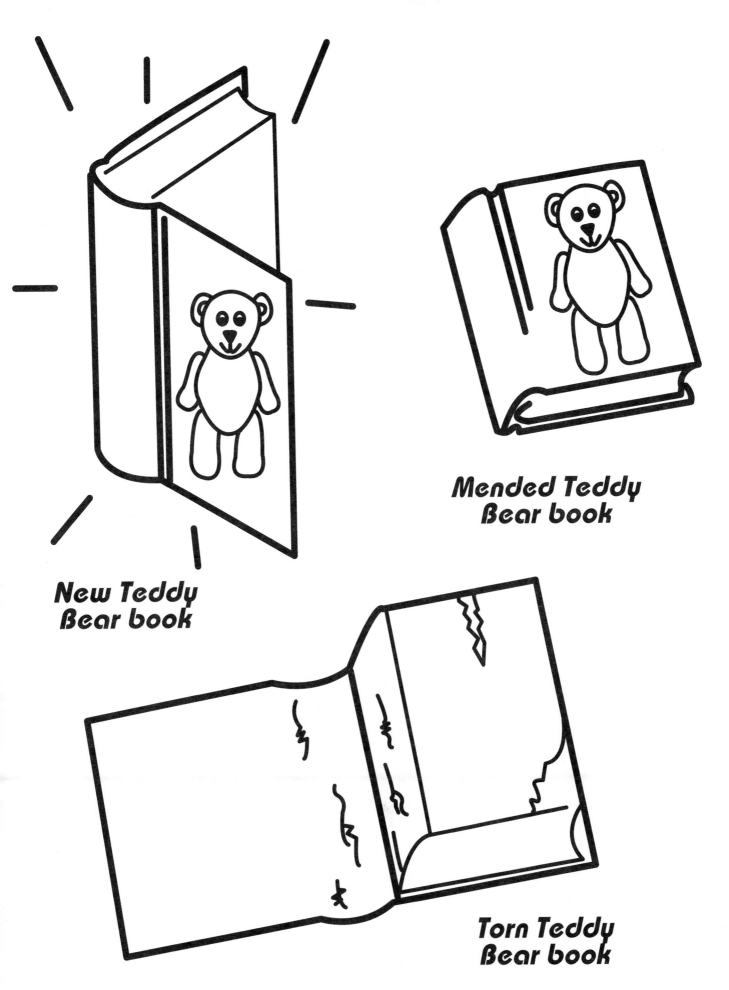

New Teddy Bear book

Mended Teddy Bear book

Torn Teddy Bear book

Tree

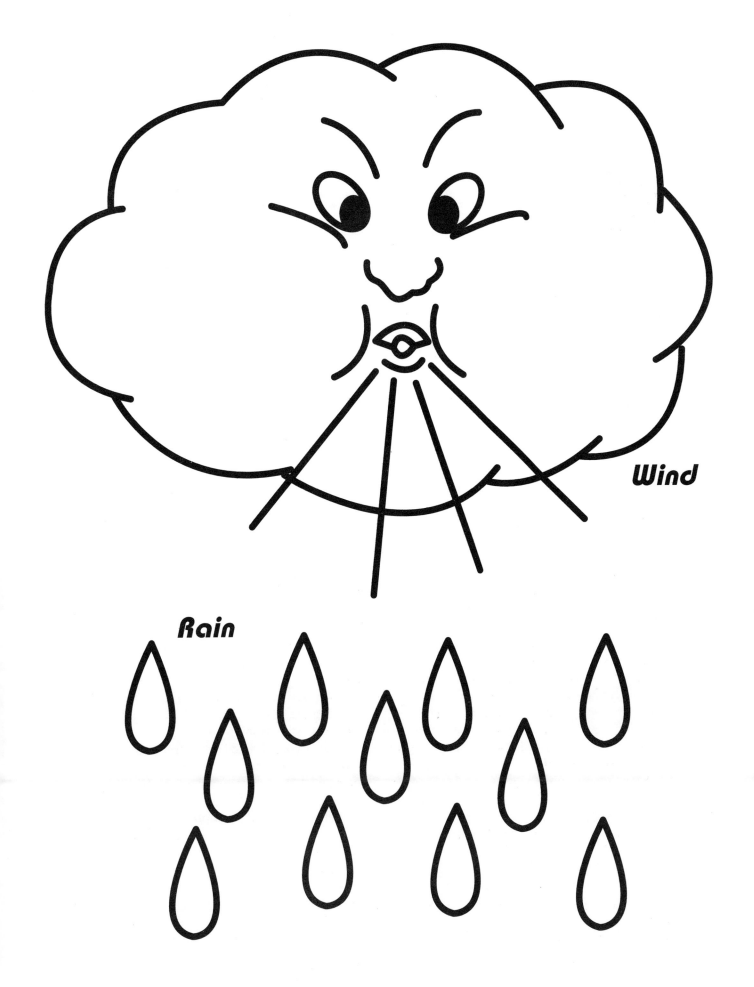

Wind

Rain

155

18 The Just Right Gift

This story is about feelings. It has some problem solving involved. This could be acted out. Children from other stories in the book can be used as patterns for classmates in this story.

Pictures needed for this story:

Happy/Sad Albert
Donny
Sara Sue
red and white checked shirt
blue pants
red cap, red socks, red suspender
shoes
teacher
ball, stuffed animal, cookies, crayons
book & scrapbook
Sara Sue's and Donny's Mother & Dad
store front
house

Albert was a new boy at school. Albert was very nicely dressed. He had on a clean red and white **checked shirt** and **blue pants**, He wore a beautiful pair of **red suspenders** and a **red cap**. His **shoes** were neatly polished and **his socks** were bright red. Albert's hair was slicked down neat as could be and he had big brown eyes and many freckles on his face. The only thing wrong was that Albert had an angry or **sad look on his face**. He just didn't look friendly.

Sara Sue went up to **Albert** and said, "Hi Albert, welcome to school."

Albert just grunted.

Donny went up to **Albert** and said, "Hi Albert, glad you're here."

Albert just grunted.

As the days went by **Albert** became very **sad-looking** because he had no friends, and he was all alone. As much as the other children tried to make friends, Albert just turned and went the other way.

Sara Sue and **Donny** decided to ignore him and went to play with their other friends.

One day Albert didn't come to school. Albert didn't come the next day either.

Sara Sue and **Donny** went to ask the **teacher** about **Albert**.

"Why isn't Albert in school?" they asked.

"Albert and his family are moving away," the teacher said. "Albert's father has a job that takes him to many different places, and they don't stay in one place very long."

"That must be very hard on Albert," Sara Sue said.

"Yes, and he never has time to make new friends," commented Donny.

"Albert never tries to make friends because if he does, he just has to leave them and move away," said the teacher.

Sara Sue and Donny knew where Albert lived so they decided to visit him before he moved away.

"We should take him a good-bye gift," said **Sara Sue**.

"We can use some of our allowance money to buy the gift," commented Donny. "What will we buy him?"

Sara Sue and **Donny** thought for a long time. They thought about a **ball**, a **stuffed animal**, some **cookies**, even **crayons**.

They went and asked their **parents**. Sara Sue's **parents** thought a **book** would be nice. Donny's **mom** and **dad** suggested a **scrapbook for mementos**.

"I like the idea of a **scrapbook**," said Sara Sue. "Maybe we could find one with pages for photos, too."

"That would be great," said Donny. "Albert could keep his memories about all the places he's lived and all the friends he's made at school in one scrapbook."

"Maybe he won't be afraid to make friends if he can look at pictures of them," said Sara Sue.

"Hurry, let's go to the **store** and find our special scrapbook-photo album," Donny said.

Sara Sue and **Donny** found the exact **scrapbook** they were seeking. They bought it with their allowance money and took it to Albert's **house**.

When Sara Sue and Donny gave Albert their gift he was very excited.

"Thank you for this great gift!" exclaimed Albert. "I'll always remember you, and I won't be afraid to make new friends because I can always look for them in my scrapbook.

Sara Sue and Donny promised to get pictures of all of their classmates to send to Albert. Albert promised to write to the whole class about his new home and his new friends at school.

Happy & sad Albert

Sara Sue

Donny

159

Donny's Mom & Dad

Store

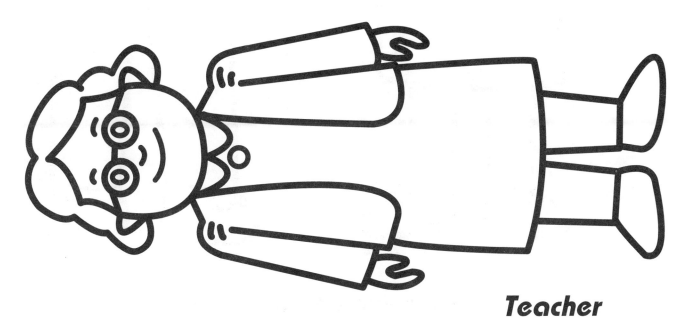

Teacher

Sara Sue's Mom & Dad

Red cap

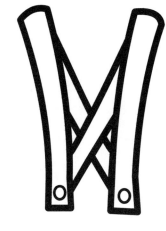

Red suspenders

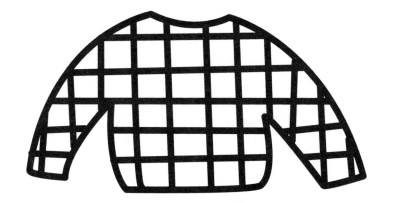

Red & white checked shirt

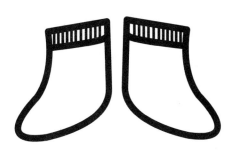

Red socks

Blue pants

Shoes

Cookies

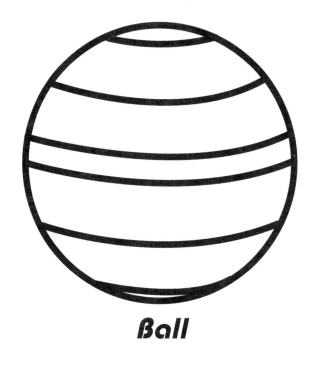

Ball

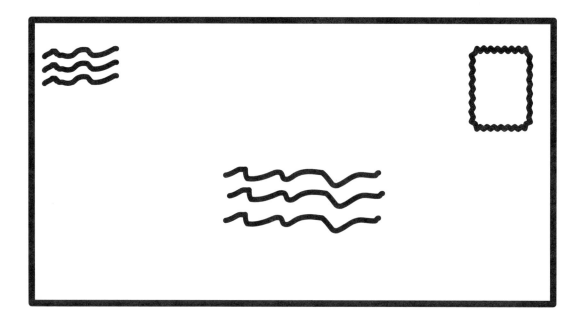

Letter

Crayons

Teddy Bear

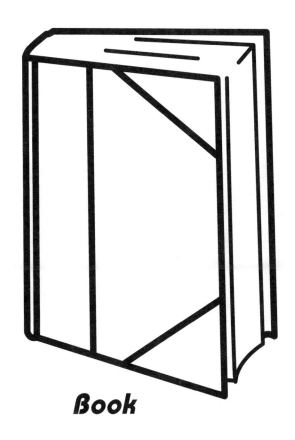

Book

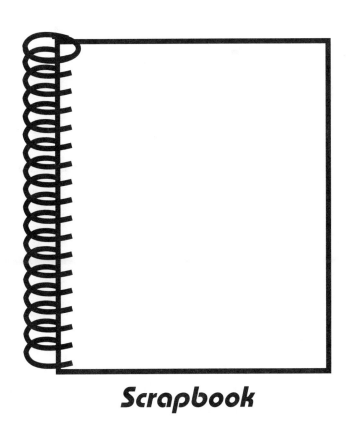

Scrapbook

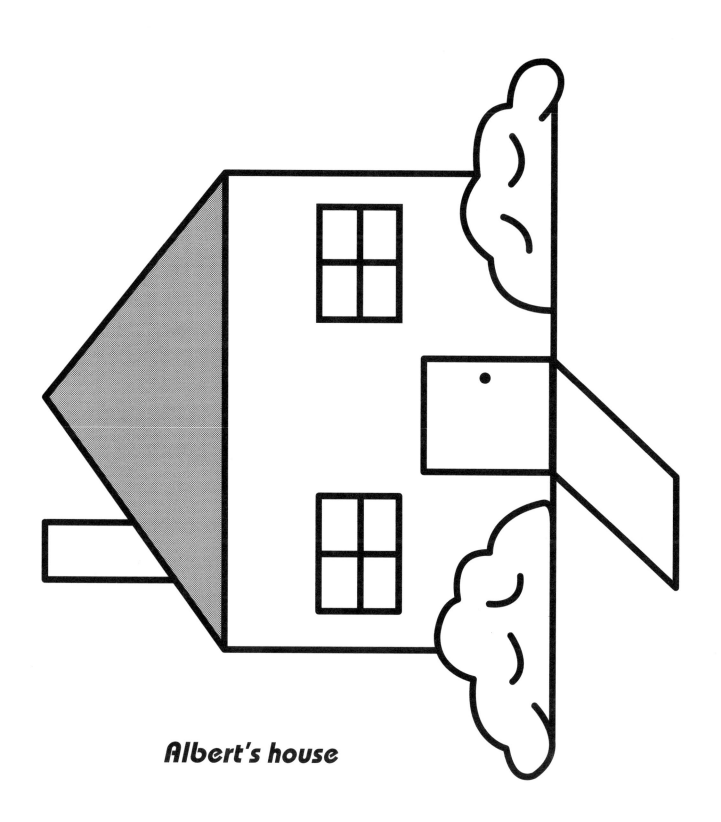

Albert's house

19 A Field Trip

This story is about libraries. Children from other stories can be used as patterns for additional students on the trip.

Pictures needed for the story:

teacher	library card
librarian	shelves of books
Willy	book box
Maxwell	table and chairs
Megan	movies & tapes
stuffed animals	
books—all sizes and colors	
atlas & encyclopedias	

On Wednesday our **kindergarten class** was getting ready for a field trip to the library.

"What's a field trip?" asked **Maxwell**.

"It's when a group leaves the classroom to visit another place," answered the **teacher**. "Today we will be visiting the library."

"What's a library?" asked **Willy**.

"I know, I know," called **Megan** excitedly. "I've been to the library with my parents for story hour. A library has lots and lots of **books on shelves** all around the room."

"Yes," said the **teacher**, "there are rooms lined with **shelves,** filled with hundreds of books, all sizes and shapes and colors."

"I can't read yet. Will I be able to get a book?" asked **Willy**.

"Yes, you will, Willy. There are many **picture books** for you to see," said the teacher.

When the children arrived at the library, they each immediately found a **chair** and sat at a **table**. The **librarian, Mrs. Appleby**, told them all about the library. She explained to them that everyone who wanted to take a book home needed a card, called a **library card**. She told them that many libraries issued a card to children entering first grade.

"I'll be in first grade next year," said **Megan**. "Now my mother takes books out for me on her card."

"That's right," said Mrs. Appleby, "Your parents may now use their card for your books."

"If you look closely at the books on the shelves you will notice a label on the spine of each book. These labels will help you find special books. Some libraries use different forms of identification on their books. I will show you which shelves hold books just right for your age group."

Mrs. Appleby took the **children** to their special section and let each child pick out two or three **books** to take back to their **tables**.

The children enjoyed looking at picture books.

"I like this book because it has lots of pictures of trucks," said Willy.

"Mine has all the nursery rhymes in it," said Megan.

When the children were finished looking at the books, they put them back in a **special box** so the librarian could replace them on the shelves later.

"Let's go to the story room now," said **Mrs. Appleby**.

The **boys** and **girls** followed the librarian and their **teacher** up some stairs, around a corner and behind some book shelves into the story room.

The story room had many **stuffed animals** and **puppets**. Mrs. Appleby even used some of them to tell her stories. As she read the stories to the children, she would hold the book up so that they could see the pictures. She even used a flannelboard to tell one of her stories.

Just before the children had to leave and go back to their school, the **librarian** explained to them that **tapes** and **movies** could be checked out with their library card as well as **books**.

"Some libraries even have special toys that can be taken out. The library has many resources for older students to use in their school studies, such as **atlases** and **encyclopedias**," said the librarian. "I hope you enjoyed your library visit. Please bring your parents and come again."

"Thank you, Mrs Appleby, we will come back," called the **children** together.

Maxwell

Willy

Teacher

Megan

Library Card

BOOKS

Book box

Librarian

170

Books of all sizes

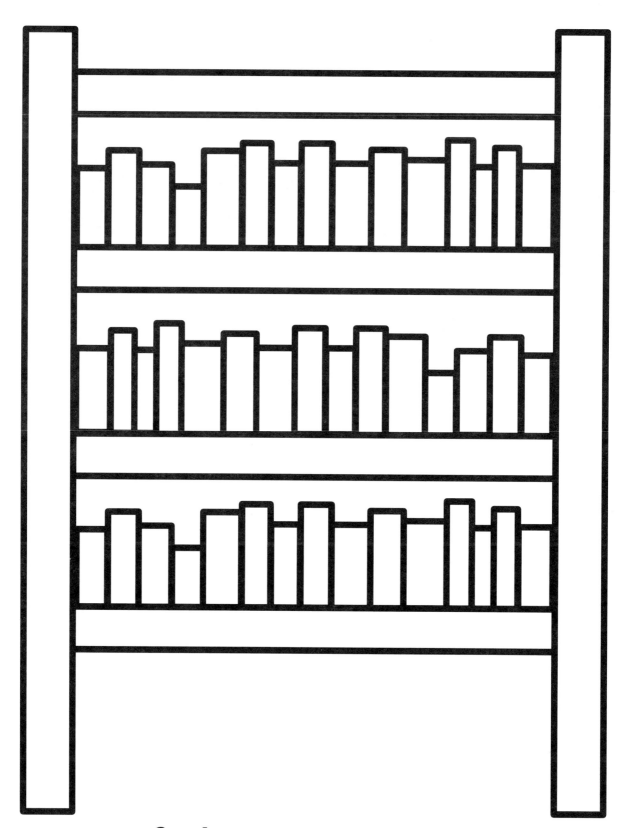

Bookcase

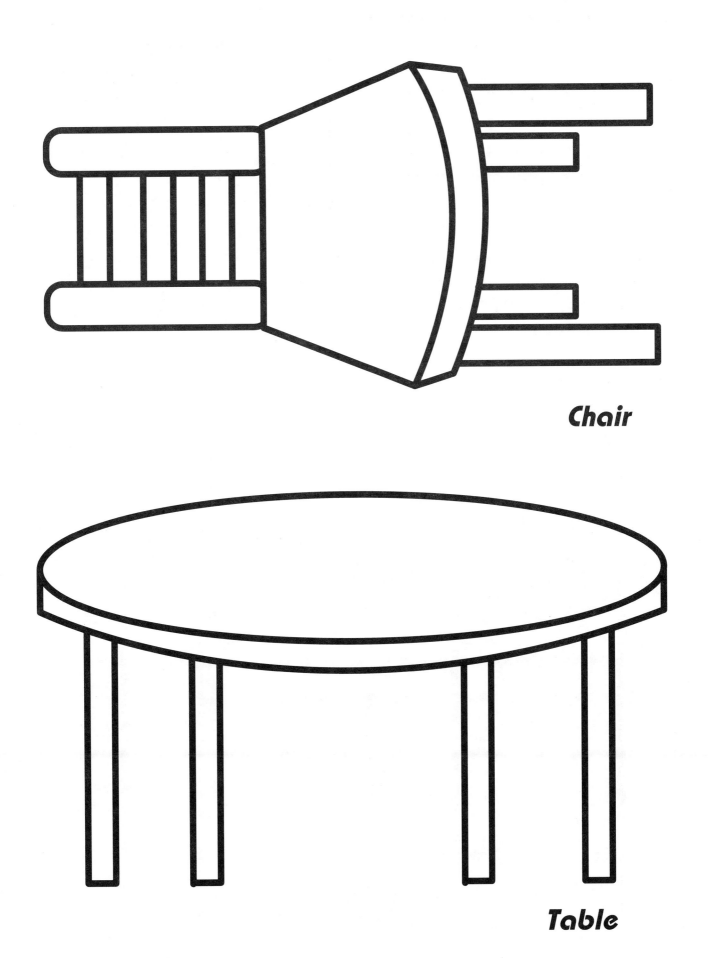

Chair

Table

173

Movies & tapes

Atlas & encyclopedias

A–E   F–J   K–O   P–T   U–Z

20 The Bake Sale

This story teaches about baking, how to find the ingredients, and some problem solving.

Pictures needed for this story:

Susan	carton of eggs
Mother	cereal box
bowl	marshmallows
flour jar	sugar jar
milk	animal & zoo cage
recipe book	cake & candy
cookies	

Susan's kindergarten class was having a bake sale in school the next day. They were going to raise money for a field trip to the **zoo**.

Susan arrived home from school all excited, "Mommy, Mommy, we need to bake a cake for my class at school", she yelled.

Her **mother** came running into the room to see what was the matter.

"What did you say, Susan?" she asked.

"Where is the recipe book?" asked Susan. "We need to bake something for my class bake sale."

Susan and her **mother** found the **recipe book** and started to look for cake recipes.

"Let's see," her mother said. "We need **flour, sugar, eggs** and **milk** to make a **cake**."

"I'll look in the kitchen and find a **bowl** to mix it in," said Susan. While **Susan** was getting the bowl out, her **mother** went to the **flour jar** and looked inside.

"We don't have any flour," said her mother. She looked in the **sugar jar**, "We don't have any sugar either."

"I'll look in the **refrigerator** and get the **milk** and **eggs**," said **Susan**. " Oh, me, oh, my. We don't have any milk or eggs either. "What shall we do?"

Susan and her **mother** started looking in the **recipe book** to find a recipe that didn't take **flour, sugar, milk** or **eggs**.

"**Cookies** need **flour, candy** needs **sugar, cakes** need **eggs** and **milk**. They all needed flour, sugar, milk and eggs. What will we do?" her mother asked.

Susan and her mother put on their thinking caps and thought and thought.

"I know, **Susan**, we will make crispy squares, they only take **cereal** and **marshmallows**," said her mother excitedly.

"I know we have **cereal** and **marshmallows**," said **Susan**.

The next day **Susan** took her **crispy squares** to school for the bake sale. The bake sale was a big success and **Susan**'s class had their trip to the **zoo**.

Mother

Susan

Cook book

Candy

Cake

Cookies

Bowl

Marshmallows

FLOUR

Flour

SUGAR

Sugar

Eggs

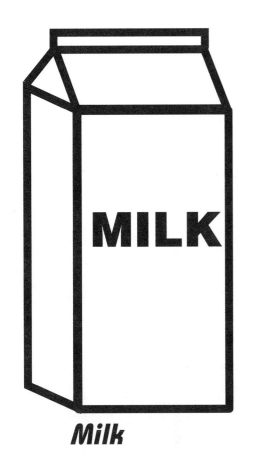

MILK

Milk

CRISP CEREAL

Cereal

Crispy treats

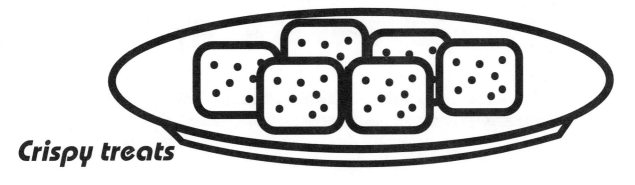

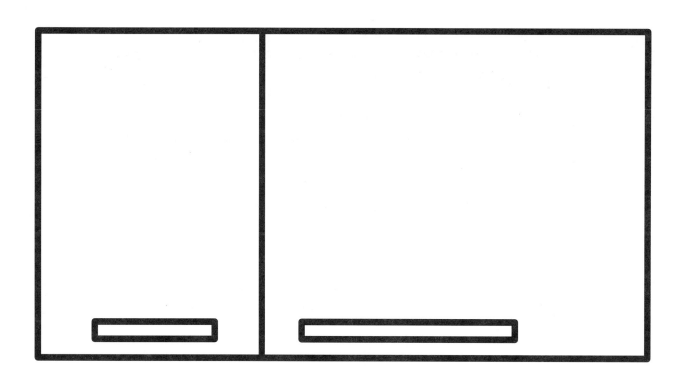

Refrigerator

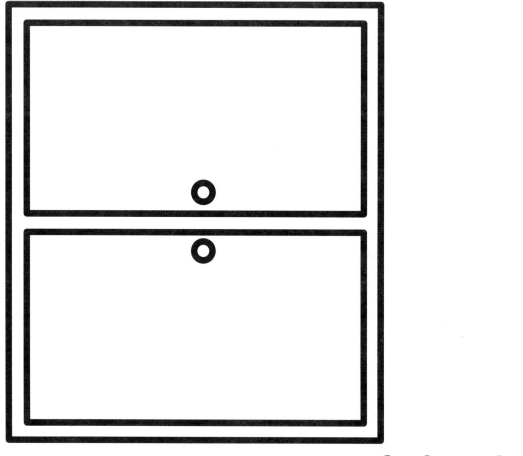

Cupboard

Cage

Elephant

21 Helping Out

This story involves some problem solving. Feelings are explained. This story may be acted out.

Pictures needed for this story:

Annabelle Rabbit	oven
Clarence Rabbit	carrots
Oscar Rabbit	trees
mother rabbit	window ledge
boy rabbit	three pies
three baby bunnies	food-clothing-wood
kitchen window	
three pie tins	
old house- new house	

The Rabbit family kitchen was a very bright, sunny room. It had bright walls and **cute ruffled curtains** at the **window**. The smell of freshly baked **carrot pies** still lingered in the air.

"Stop thief," yelled **Annabelle Rabbit**. This was the second time this week that a pie had been taken from her window sill. Mother Rabbit (called Annabelle by her husband and friends, and called Mother by her son) had spent all morning baking pies. You see rabbit families like carrot pies. Mother Rabbit had rolled out the pie crust just the right size to fit the **pie pan**. She had washed and cut up the **carrots** and put them in the pan covering the bottom crust. Then she had poured some sweet honey over them and covered this with the top crust. With a fork, Mother Rabbit had put a few slits in the top crust so the steam could escape while they were baking. She made sure the temperature in **oven** had been set just right to bake the pies.

Mother Rabbit had made **three pies**. One pie was for a neighbor family whose mother was sick. One pie was for the church bazaar that was being held that very evening. The third pie was for her family. Mother Rabbit had just taken the pies from the oven and put them on the window ledge to cool. She still had on her **pot holder mittens** to protect her hands from the hot pie dish. The pie thief must have been hiding under the kitchen window because he took the pie very quickly. Mother Rabbit got a good look at the boy as he ran away carrying the pie.

"He's just a child," said Mother Rabbit. "Why would he need to steal a pie? Do you suppose he is hungry or just doing it to be bad or mischievous?"

Father Rabbit (or Clarence, as his wife and friends called him) heard his wife yell and came to the kitchen to see what was wrong. **Little Oscar** Rabbit, Annabell and Clarence's son, also came into the kitchen to find out why his mother had yelled. Even a small bird singing in the tree by the window flew away because of all the commotion.

"Let's hurry and see if we can find out where the boy is going with our pie?" said **Mother Rabbit**. Mother, father, and son all ran out the door and started to follow the pie thief.

He had gotten a good start, so he was far into the woods hidden by the **trees**. Every once in a while he could be seen slipping behind a tree, but before too long the Rabbit family had almost caught up with him. They could run faster because the thief had to be careful not to drop the pie as he ran.

Then, just when they came to the top of a hill and looked around—the boy thief was gone. He seemed to have disappeared. The only thing in sight was a broken-down **old house**.

Annabelle, **Clarence** and **Oscar** went to the old **house** and looked inside. There were **three small rabbit babies**, the **boy** who had taken the **carrot pie** and their **mother**. They looked scared as the strangers came into the room. It only took Annabelle, Clarence and Oscar one look to see why the boy had taken the pie. The house was badly in need of repair, there was almost no furniture, no food and no wood for the stove. This poor family needed help.

Their father was gone (maybe the one Mr. McGregor caught), the mother had to stay home and care for the babies. They had no money and no one to keep the home in repair.

"I'm sorry I took your pie," the frightened **boy** cried.

"I think your family needs our help," said Annabelle Rabbit.

Annabelle, Clarence and **Oscar** Rabbit went to their friends and neighbors for help. Everyone came to help. **New porch steps were built**, **food** and **clothing** was donated, even **wood** for the stove was contributed. Best of all, the boy who had taken the pie was given a part- time job and could earn some money to help his family. The **boy** and **Oscar** became good friends and played together.

The next time **Annabelle Rabbit** baked **carrot pies** and put them on the **window sill**, they stayed there.

Trees

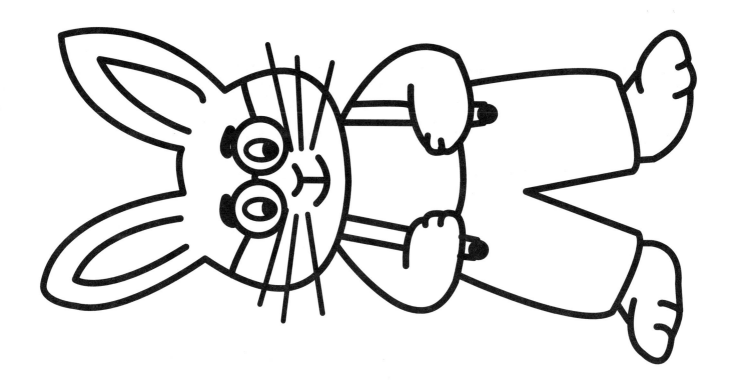

Clarence

Annabelle

184

Mother & babies

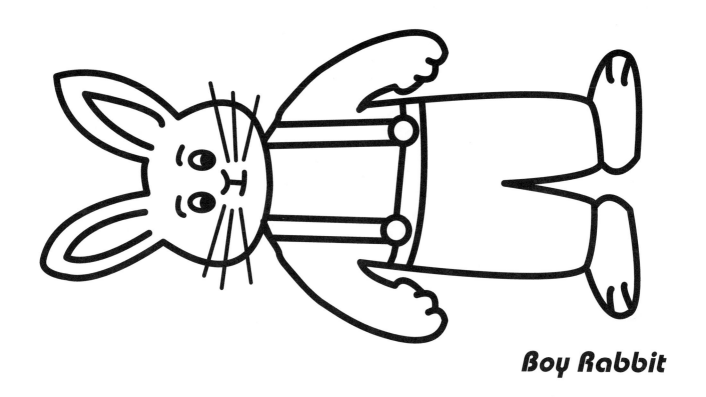

Boy Rabbit

Oscar

Mother & babies

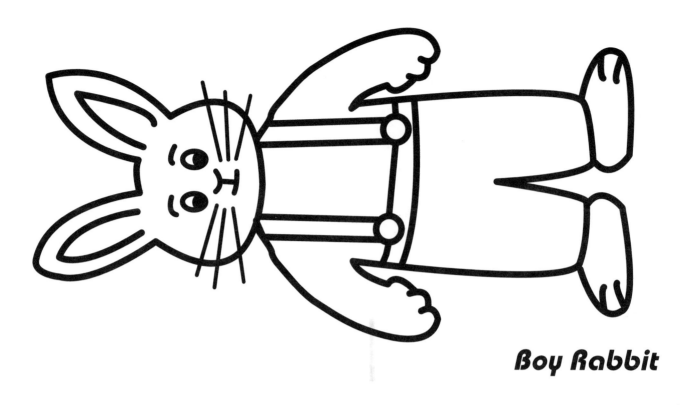

Boy Rabbit

Oscar

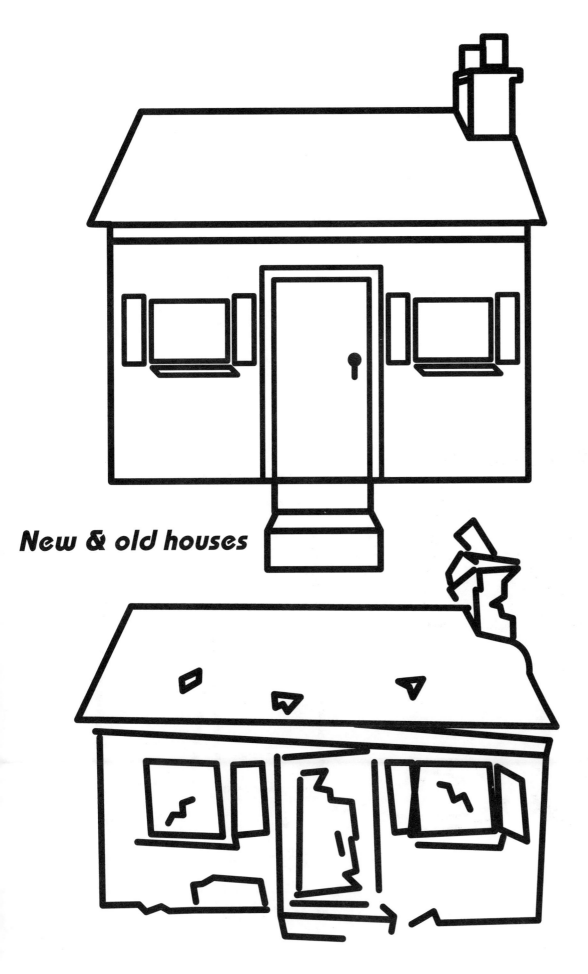

New & old houses

Clothing

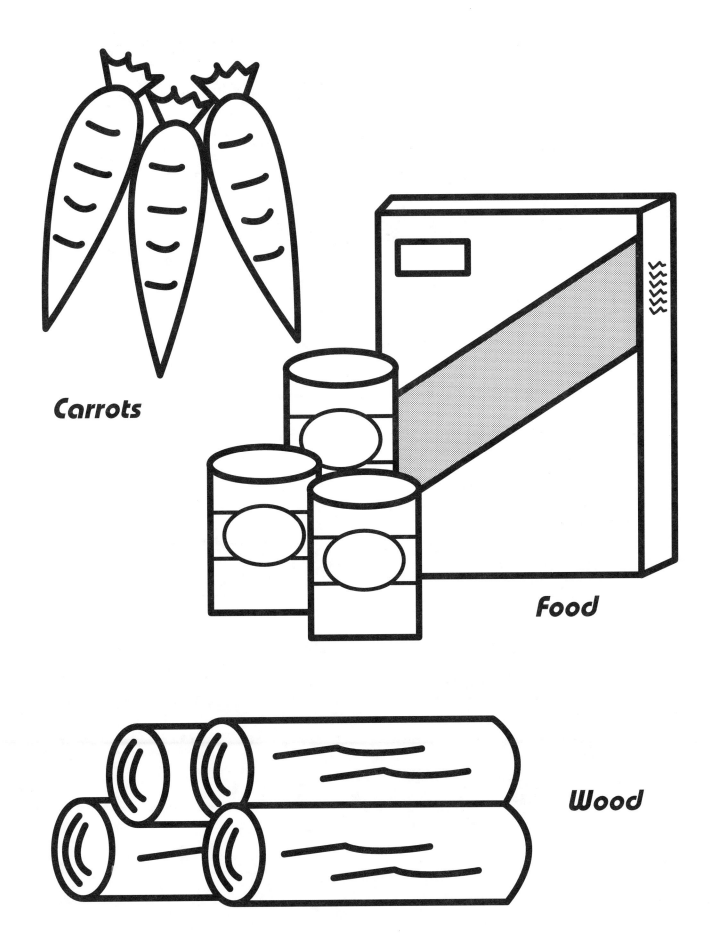

Carrots

Food

Wood

189

Oven

Oven mit

Pie tins

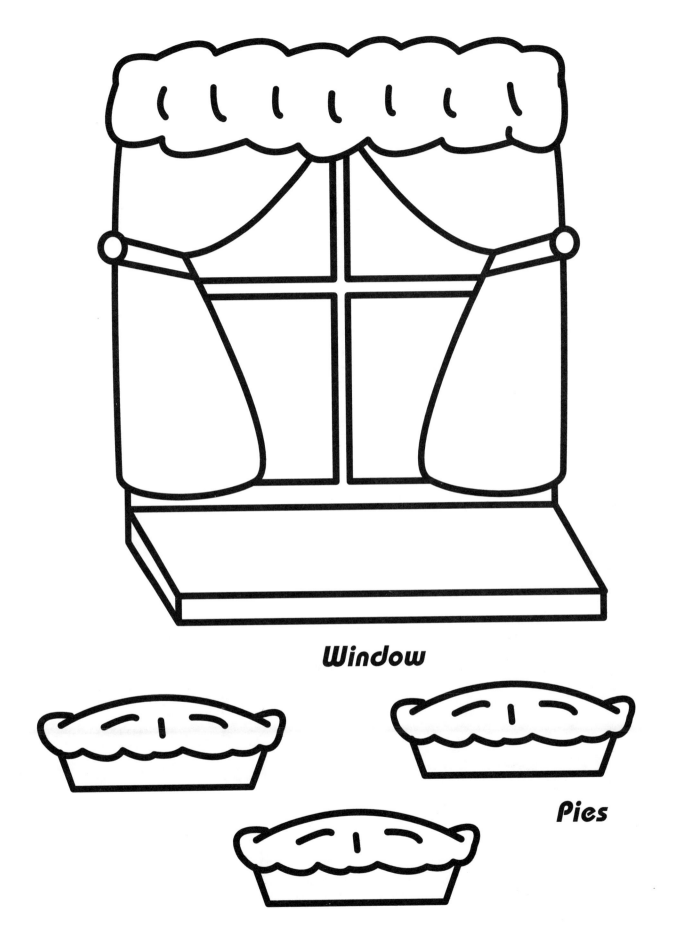

Window

Pies